REMEMBERING

Lewiston-Auburn

ON THE MIGHTY

ANDROSCOGGIN

REMEMBERING

Lewiston-Auburn

ON THE MIGHTY

ANDROSCOGGIN

River Views

DAVID A. SARGENT

Charleston   London

THE
History
PRESS

Published by The History Press
Charleston, SC 29403
www.historypress.net

Images are courtesy of the author unless otherwise noted.

First published 2010

Manufactured in the United States

ISBN 978.1.59629.366.3

Library of Congress Cataloging-in-Publication Data

Sargent, David A.
Remembering Lewiston-Auburn on the mighty Androscoggin : river views / David A.
Sargent.
p. cm.
ISBN 978-1-59629-366-3
1. Lewiston (Me.)--History. 2. Auburn (Me.)--History. 3. Androscoggin River Region
(N.H. and Me.)--History. 4. Lewiston (Me.)--Social life and customs. 5. Auburn (Me.)-
-Social life and customs. 6. Auburn (Me.)--Economic conditions. 7. Lewiston (Me.)--
Economic conditions. I. Title.
F29.L63S27 2010
974.1'82--dc22
2010021979

Contents

CONTENTS

INTRODUCTION

River Views

My river views are from Echo Farm, my family's farm on the Auburn banks of Maine's mighty Androscoggin River. From our riverside fields, I can see into a remarkable past, and I believe I can see a wonderful future.

Androscoggin County was barely ten years old when the Civil War ended in 1865. My great-grandfather was headed home to Auburn, to a young bride and a farmhouse newly built for the family on what is now North River Road.

Family history has come full circle for me in recent years, as my wife, Judy, and I had an opportunity to move back to my boyhood home. Furthermore, I have had an opportunity to write about Androscoggin County's first 150 years and its exciting steps into the twenty-first century. Most of the material in this book was published in my twice-monthly columns in the daily *Lewiston Sun Journal*, and my research draws heavily from the *Journal*'s pages, which date back to 1847.

No, this is not history. I think this book should be about all kinds of interesting things that have happened, how and why they were important to us and how they affect our lives now and in the future. Come to think of it, that is history, but let's just think of it as some stories I'd like to pass on to you.

It was probably the Fourth of July in about 1917 when my father, Walter Sargent, struck a patriotic pose as a hay wagon arrived at the barn.

What kind of stories do I seek out? Many focus on the Androscoggin River itself. It went from a pristine condition in which salmon thrived to a seriously polluted industrial waste receiver. It's now on the rebound, and nearby residents can again enjoy its recreational benefits and promise for the future.

We have legends of Native American raids and tragedies at the Great Falls. The stuff of legends is also present in the courageous men, from laborers to industrial giants, who built dams on the river, created canals and put up massive mills that still promise to influence our destiny.

Do you know about the corn factories or the bean canneries? Our North River Road farm had a small role in those little-known ventures when canned goods were relatively new.

Years ago, the week after Labor Day brought the Maine State Fair to Lewiston Fairgrounds. It featured harness racing and agricultural exhibitions, not to mention the World of Mirth amusements. Every time I hear sirens across the river on Lewiston's upper Main Street, I think of the wailing siren that hawked the carnival's popular daredevil motorcycle motodrome.

The towering boiler-room stack at Bates Mill can be seen from many points in the Twin Cities.

Now, the state fair is gone, but the annual Great Falls Balloon Festival in August brings tens of thousands of people from near and far to the banks of the Androscoggin in the heart of our Twin Cities of Lewiston and Auburn.

Since I have no credentials as a historian, except curiosity and a love for this place, I am indebted to many people who have collected and generously shared the facts (and sometimes fiction) we'll explore. There is one particular writer who was familiar to readers of the tabloid-sized magazine section of the *Lewiston Evening Journal* every Saturday. The byline of Edith Andrews on weekly columns meant that readers would find unique insight into a local person or place. Her byline (after later marriages) appeared as Edith Labbie and Edith Dolan. She was my aunt,

The magnificent Saints Peter and Paul Basilica rises above homes of many Franco-American residents whose ancestors helped build it.

and her enthusiasm for life and writing was always an inspiration to me. I also have been inspired by the poetic talents of my father, Walter F. Sargent, and my brother, Jim, and have benefited from the assistance and encouragement of my wife, Judy.

To begin, I would like to sketch the Lewiston-Auburn (L-A) I know today. Some local buildings and events have disappeared, some have changed and some are brand-new and bright with promise.

Although shopping malls have replaced downtown streets that were once crowded with shoppers, we now have several parks and plazas for music by all kinds of bands. There is a beautiful riverwalk in downtown L-A, and there's Thorncrag Nature Sanctuary in Lewiston. Places to eat are everywhere, from hot dog carts to upscale dining in a restored historic building.

Saints Peter and Paul Basilica is an architectural masterpiece with a rose window replica from the Chartres Cathedral and one of the most magnificent organs in New England. The former St. Mary's Church in Lewiston's Little Canada is now a beautiful concert hall.

The river brought water power, which ran the early mill machinery and gave birth to a textile industry that attracted our Franco-American population. Didn't big developments always depend on the convergence of resources and opportunity? Museum L/A tells the stories of workers in mills, shoe factories and brickyards.

The arts and sports are alive and well here. Music, dance and drama are found at the Public Theatre, the Community Little Theatre, Bates College, the Franco-American Heritage Center and many other venues. And hockey continues its long tradition as the top sports attraction. The Androscoggin Bank Colisée, formerly the Central Maine Civic Center on Birch Street in Lewiston, is where hockey fans catch the excitement of a MAINEiacs game. That team comprises high school students from Canada and other countries, and it's the only U.S. franchise of the Quebec Major Junior Hockey League, which has produced a number of National Hockey League greats.

That's what we look like today. In the following pages, I hope to show you some of what you might have seen in years gone by.

PART I

Early Industry

THE POWER OF WATER

Long before production of electricity was the goal of harnessing rivers, the fortunes of people along the Androscoggin depended on water power. Even before water surged through the Lewiston canal system to turn wheels of industry, there were other important applications for that age-old source of energy.

Hundreds of sawmills, gristmills and fulling mills once dotted the water-rich landscape of Androscoggin County. Those mills could thrive on some pretty small streams; sometimes all that was needed was dependable flow through little more than a ditch.

I found documentation of these many mills in *History of Androscoggin County*, edited by Georgia Drew Merrill in 1891. It's a large gilt-edged book with pages now coming loose from the binding because generations of our family have spent hours leafing through it.

The book's entries for the Town of Wales (bordering Lewiston) illustrate some of the early but short-lived enterprises: "During the first 12 or 15 years of settlement, the settlers were obliged to carry their bags of corn and grain on their shoulders 20 miles to the nearest mill." They followed blazed trails through the forest.

Lewiston's canal system brought water power to the large brick textile mills that thrived in the city for many years.

The only gristmill "was built by Joseph Maxwell on a small stream in the eastern part of the town, near his dwelling." The first sawmill "was built by Daniel M. Labree on a small stream on his home farm where he could saw some boards, shingles, etc., for a few weeks each in the spring and fall."

If any stream could turn a water wheel, there was a good chance that Maine entrepreneurs were capturing that force of nature and making some money from it. Some set up water-driven saws that cut with a slow but sure up-and-down motion.

Gristmills also captured the power of water. They turned massive round millstones that rolled over a farmer's grain, crushing it into flour or meal.

Another kind of local operation was the fulling mill. Fulling was a step in cloth-making (particularly wool) to get rid of oils and dirt. Once again, labor-saving water power was used to move wooden hammers that beat the cloth.

The old volume of history also yielded some unexpected information about a rather tempestuous side of mill ownership and operation.

Moses Little, who played an early and vital role in Lewiston's history, built a large woolen mill next to the falls in 1809. It stood at the present Cowan and Libbey Mill location and was the first to have a sawmill, gristmill and fulling mill under one roof.

In the spring of 1814, fire destroyed the mill, and the old history book asserts, "These mills were undoubtedly burned by the torch of the incendiary," meaning an arsonist. Neither motive nor perpetrator is spelled out, but the account continues, "There was unquestionably much feeling in the community against Mr. Little."

In a letter to a friend, Little said that his son, Michael, was urging him to rebuild. He wrote:

> *If the people think the mills will be safe from the base incendiary, who has no more regard for one man than another, I will, with the assistance of the people, make one more trial to rebuild them. But I should like to have the timber cut on the old of the moon, that if it should be preserved from fire it might be more durable.*

(There was a belief that wood cut in the moon's last quarter would dry better.)

Maybe his requirement really did lead to a superior product, because the rebuilt mill operated until 1850.

MILLS THAT BUILT L-A

Dozens of small mills of all types once dotted the banks of nearby waterways, and most of them were lost to fire or flood. A few thrived, and others came and went quickly, but each played a critical role in this area's development.

The first woolen mill in the United States was built in Gray, just south of Auburn. The owner had learned the manufacturing process in England, but that country forbade export of the technology. Samuel Mayall smuggled himself out of Britain and started his business in Maine in 1791.

Other area mills were recalled in an article written nearly fifty years ago by Dick Murray, a frequent contributor to the *Lewiston Journal* magazine section.

Murray said the first mill near L-A's present business centers was on Auburn's Foundry Brook, where water originating in springs on outer Summer Street and Lake Street flowed to the "Big Falls." That neighborhood produced a succession of sawmills, gristmills and tanneries and the once prosperous Penley Packing Company.

The Dillinghams built these early mills, Murray said, and Edward Little had a small carpet factory that did a sizeable business. Knight Street in that area later had a gristmill owned by J.E. Tibbetts, and it is said to have ground sixty thousand bushels of grain annually.

The Stevens Mills area of Auburn got its name from the enterprises of Jacob Stevens in the late 1700s. He made good use of a thirty-foot drop over two miles of the outlet brook of Taylor Pond. About 1800, Jacob's

Squire Edward Little played a major role in early Auburn's history. Among his many contributions was his gift of Lewiston Falls Academy, which became Edward Little High School.

sons, Moses and Parker, changed the original gristmill into a sawmill that turned out clapboards, laths and shingles into the 1860s. Later, the site produced cardboard and fiberboard products.

The Stevens family had another mill farther down Taylor Brook. Features of the dam and original gristmill are still easily seen where Minot Avenue crosses Taylor Brook. That mill dated back almost to the Revolutionary War.

Stetson Brook and the Sabattus Pond outlet also provided water power long ago, and the Nezinscot River at Turner powered many industries, including the Priscilla Rug Company.

Mills came in all sizes and were used for many purposes, and the waterways of Androscoggin County have witnessed a treasure of historical lore about them.

"HISTORY BECOMES THE FUTURE"

Elliott Epstein, a local attorney, knows the need and the opportunities for saving important pieces of L-A's industrial past. A few years ago, he laid the foundation for rescuing textile mill records, machinery and nearly forgotten stories of the workers. He and some volunteers spent a lot of time moving big pieces of textile machinery that seemed destined for a scrap heap. That's how Museum L/A, a small but promising museum in the empty space of the historic Bates Mill, took shape, with a staff led by the boundless enthusiasm of executive director Rachel DesGrosseilliers.

Building a new museum is much more than a desk job for DesGrosseilliers. She has gathered all kinds of artifacts for the textile industry and shoemaking displays from the cities' old mills, shoe factories and even brickyards.

In the massive and mostly empty Bates Mill, she tells how she "literally went into some of the dump trucks." She and two former millworkers, who were seventy-six and seventy-nine years old, pulled out job descriptions, procedure manuals, patterns and swatches of material that showed the woven patterns.

"Up on the fourth floor there was a cabinet that was all boarded up, so I took a crowbar and opened it up and…Oh, my God! It's the pigeon-hole cabinet [now displayed in the museum] that has all the old patterns."

She described her amazement when she got her first look at the mill's old vault, a large space—maybe ten feet by twenty feet—filled floor to ceiling with old documents.

You never know what you'll find. You never know where it will lead or what effect it will have. That's why, DesGrosseilliers says, "History becomes the future."

When she thinks about things that may already be gone forever, she says she pictures box after box of Bates bedspreads that were sold off for "practically nothing." Once in a while, one of them turns up, such as a rare original Queen Elizabeth bedspread in the Wedgewood design.

She had been told how that design, decades ago, went through the process required for all commercial goods allowed to carry the British monarchy's seal of approval. She learned how every detail of the design was considered. Finally, a courier arrived at the Bates Mill with the approved pattern inside a locked briefcase that was handcuffed to the courier's wrist.

DesGrosseilliers knows perfectly well that history is not just about things. That's why she places high value on the oral history phase of Museum L/A's development.

A woman who was interviewed for Museum L/A's oral history project remembered her youth as a worker in the mill. She told how she worked a day shift and then went home so a sister could go off to work the second shift. In the next part of the story, she gives the kind of detail that only the people who live it can pass on. The young girl would go home and take off her shoes; her sister would put them on and head back to the mill in the only pair of shoes the girls had.

In community presentations, Epstein told about farmers many years ago who needed extra work through the long winters, so they worked in mills and factories. He talked about the Irish potato famine that brought desperate families to our shores. Many Irishmen came here to dig the canals. He explained ingenious mechanisms that took the power of water flowing through those canals and—by cogged wheels, shafts, pulleys and belts—brought it throughout the sprawling mills. And he talked about the vital role of Franco-American millworkers.

Epstein gives perspective to Lewiston's textile history when he explains how the vision of Boston financier Benjamin Bates led to the canal and mill construction here just before the Civil War. With access to cotton in the South disrupted, the price went from twelve cents to a dollar a pound. It was boom time in L-A as military orders came in for tent cloth, uniforms and boots.

In 1857, Bates Manufacturing Co. was turning out 5.7 million yards of cloth a year. During the Civil War and up to 1867, the seven mills of Lewiston produced $34 million worth of cotton and woolen goods, Epstein said.

Statistics, yes, but presented with Epstein's enthusiasm, we can grasp the excitement that must have prevailed here at that time. "We're different from other mill towns," Epstein affirms. "We held on longer."

THE VIEW FROM MOUNT DAVID

There's a piece of property in Lewiston that's often regarded as a special gem. For many generations, a relatively modest rise of land known as Mount David has drawn people to its summit for a breathtaking view of the surrounding city. The hill's rugged ledge and scraggly trees are much the same today as they were more than one hundred years ago, although the residential streets on three sides and the Bates College campus to the east have changed greatly over time.

Rose D. Nealley recalled the area in a 1938 article written for the *Lewiston Journal*. She described the land as "a mountain by courtesy," but its height offered area residents views of the "silver ribbon of the Androscoggin," Mount Gile in Auburn, the Hebron hills and, on a clear day, the White Mountains. She also wrote of wild red columbine, gray squirrels "nearly as tame as kittens" and "the lovely fairy-like towers of the new Saints Peter and Paul Church." The Vatican elevated that magnificent structure to the status of basilica in May 2006.

In the early 1800s, Lewiston's Main Street was a wagon trail that passed several large farms. Among them was the property of Amos Davis, whose farmhouse stood at the corner of Main and Whipple Streets. It was "a substantial, stately mansion," she wrote. The farm's barns and cattle sheds stood on the opposite side of the road, and orchards flourished a bit to the north where Frye Street now runs near the base of Mount David.

Davis had four children. It was for David, the youngest, that he named the hill. David's Mountain was a pasture for sheep and horses.

Nealley wrote that "somewhere at the end of Frye Street near Main there was a huge potato hole capable of containing as many as one hundred bushels of potatoes at one time. When there were no potatoes in it, the sheep would huddle there to sleep."

The Free Baptist meetinghouse stood at what is now the corner of Main Street and Mountain Avenue at the northwest side of Mount David. Nealley described how the building was moved in 1838 nearly all the way down Main Street. It was said that it took seventy-five yoke of oxen to move the old church. Farmers from miles around loaned their oxen for the occasion, Nealley said. They placed the church on a plot of land near the present B. Peck building.

There was once a house said to have been built by Roland Patterson halfway up Mount David. It burned, and by the early 1900s, few people remembered it. Only a few foundation stones remain.

At the summit, a cairn was built to support a map of landmarks under glass for the benefit of hikers, although vandals and weather eventually ruined the original map. The garnets that once studded the ledges have also disappeared in the hands of gem collectors.

Nealley's account follows several branches of the Davis family through the birth of two daughters of David Davis and the subsequent mountain ownership by the Wakefield heirs, who bequeathed the mountain to Bates College. That institution has done much for the preservation of the wonderful height of land that figures prominently in Bates College lore.

Only a few years ago, Mount David was the location of a remarkable event. Bates College's Robinson Players staged their annual Shakespeare production—*Macbeth*—in the open air on Mount David. An article in the *Bates Student Icon* in 1996 quoted the director, Bates senior Gregory Arata, as saying that the site was geologically reminiscent of the play's highland setting.

"It's Scotland up at the top, it's brilliant with the rocks and moss and sticks. It's both beautiful, yet a wasteland—a barren plain of nothing."

Gregory Stoddard, one of the actors, said that "the environment is the set." He said the play would be "eerie, scary and bloody," ending appropriately at sunset.

In distinct contrast to generations of tranquil nature hikes and family picnics, the action reverberated off the rock all around the audience members, who hiked up the hill and sat on blankets on two days in May for a unique show.

THE REMARKABLE W.S. LIBBEY

Bricks and mortar. We pile them up, and sooner or later, we knock them down.

The Libbey Mill in Lewiston, next to the Great Falls of the Androscoggin River, has been reduced to rubble by the wrecking balls after fires gutted the empty but once proud structure.

The history and economic role of each mill in L-A is significant, and the details are easily found in local libraries. However, one man who left his name on a mill played a particularly dynamic part in L-A history. Industrialist is the short but unexciting label that usually identifies Winfield Scott Libbey. I would add adventurer, because W.S. Libbey found international inspiration for the many benefits he brought to the Twin Cities.

I worked with descendants of W.S. Libbey several years ago to document that remarkable man's life.

He was born in 1851 in Avon, and his father, Asa Libbey, soon moved to West Waterville, where he farmed.

Between farm life and a lavish executive's office, Scott's life bristled with excitement. Around 1870, he learned telegraphy by watching a train depot operator, and it landed him a job in Auburn. He worked elsewhere but returned to Lewiston in 1873. For sixty-five dollars a month, he tapped out and received messages for Western Union at 14 Lisbon Street. He gained some fame for taking six thousand words of a presidential address telegraphed in Morse code without a break.

Around this time, he courted Annie E. Shaw, daughter of the agent of Lisbon's Farnsworth Mill. They married in 1877, and they lived frugally. Money went into a Lincoln Street tenement house Scott bought as an investment. In 1880, they began building a fine house at Sabattus and Nichols Streets.

A first son died of diphtheria within a month of birth, but two more sons and two daughters completed the family. However, Annie's journals, which she kept for fifty-three years, told of one medical crisis after another.

Scott's insatiable interests took him far and wide while Annie kept the home going. He went to North Dakota by train, and when the train slowed, he jumped off and backpacked until he found a spot to build a shack and stake a claim. He soon sold that land, and with his profits, he set out for Bogotá, Colombia. He bought stock in a silver mine, but it was another short-lived and disappointing venture. Scott returned to Lewiston.

On advice from his father-in-law, he bought a small cotton mill in North Auburn and a woolen mill in Vassalboro, near Augusta, that required much time and travel.

Meanwhile, Annie was doing mountains of wash, baking pies a dozen at a time on a woodstove and still finding time to make the family's clothing. One record shows that Scott paid her twenty-five cents for making him a pair of pants.

Success was on their doorstep when Scott purchased the Cumberland Woolen Mill in Lewiston with the financial backing of Henry M. Dingley, son of a Maine governor and congressman.

First chartered as the Lewiston Falls Cotton Mill Company, the old mill's looms first started up in 1846 under ownership of the Lewiston Water Power Company and, later, the Franklin Company. It was 46 feet wide, 102 feet long and five stories high, but over the years, it underwent some expansions. After initial success and then a mostly

Cowan Mill (left) and Lincoln Mill, later the Libbey Mill, are gone, but they stood on the Lewiston side of the Great Falls until recently.

idle period from 1884 to 1893, Libbey and Dingley purchased the mill. Under their leadership, exceptional changes came to Lewiston and surrounding areas.

Business expansion followed, including the acquisition, around 1890, of the empty Lincoln Mill (built in 1845 and soon to be called W.S. Libbey Co.). There had been a bumper crop of potatoes in Aroostook County, and Scott Libbey bought carloads of surplus potato starch. He stored it in the old mill, sold it at a profit and bought new machinery for the mill.

Libbey and Dingley replaced the mill's water-powered machinery with electric motors. Before long, they were building Deer Rips Dam on the Androscoggin River to generate more power. That was in 1902, about twenty years before the big Gulf Island Dam was constructed.

Electrical power led to the development of the Lewiston-to-Portland Interurban trolley line. It was Libbey's proudest achievement, but he died

Interurban Trolley Arbutus No. 10 made the first Lewiston-to-Portland Interurban trip, but the line's principal builder died a month before the inaugural run.

just two months before the inaugural run of the trolley in 1914. The trolleys eventually disappeared as automobiles took over the roads.

The old mill's most notable physical features were the two towers where stairways of peg construction took the workers to the upper floors, according to Kevin Juskewitch of Lewiston, who corresponded with me a few years ago about the Libbey Mill. He described Scott Libbey's ornate office. He said it had a painted ceiling, tiled floor, brass fixtures, mahogany woodwork with gold foil decoration and a broad fireplace with a massive mantle.

There also was an opera house in the mill, and the last performance at that venue was not so long ago. L/A Arts presented Doug Varone and Dancers in a program called *A Momentary Order* there on October 3, 1992.

Juskewitch also informed me about many of the Libbey Mill's later products: Golden Fleece woolen blankets and other brands for hotels and institutions produced into the 1960s. These brands included Viking, Trojan, North Cape, Polar, Sunshine and Touraine.

Lewiston has several more large mills with familiar names like Bates, Pepperell, Hill, Androscoggin and Continental. They still stand and serve purposes from warehousing to light manufacturing. The Bates

Mill has seen the most extensive restoration and renovation for offices and restaurants. There also were buildings that once housed large shoe factories and textile mills in Auburn, and these have been converted into apartments.

Whether we mourn the loss of old mills or hail the preservation of buildings such as the historic Dominican Block on Lewiston's Lincoln Street (currently under renovation), the significance of these structures lies with the people who passed through them. They echo with so many remarkable stories of ordinary and extraordinary people.

ARA CUSHMAN'S SHOE FACTORY

I have a lot of old postcards, and I often think of them as the original form of texting. One card I looked at recently has a penny Benjamin Franklin stamp. It was mailed on May 14, 1909, and it went from Auburn to Lewiston with a short message saying basically, "I'm feeling fine." It was the one-hundred-year-old version of text messaging, but on many levels, it says so much more with its view of long ago.

The picture on this particular card shows one of the area's largest buildings of the early 1900s: the Cushman-Hollis Shoe Factory, which stood on Court Street in Auburn next to the railroad track crossing, now an intersection of a four-lane bypass route.

When Ara Cushman built this four-story brick structure in 1868, it was said to be the largest shoe factory in Maine. There were additions through the years, and before long it gained a reputation as the nation's largest shoe factory under one roof.

Business must have been good, because in 1873 Cushman donated land at Elm and Pleasant Streets for construction of a building by the First Universalist Parish of Auburn, according to the church's website. Its cost was to be no more than $30,000.

Thanks to Ralph Skinner's book, *Auburn 1869–1969: 100 Years a City*, and information by Laurie Haynes St. Pierre in the Androscoggin Historical Society's sesquicentennial book, we learn that Cushman

A postcard shows the north side of Auburn's Court Street. Stately elm trees gave the old Elm Hotel its name.

experimented in the 1870s with some new ideas in footwear fashion. Around 1876, he began making a canvas-topped shoe with a leather sole.

A financial depression in 1893 hit the Ara Cushman Company hard. It never rebounded to its early success before the founder died in 1910. However, his son, Charles Cushman, joined with a shoemaker from Boston, John H. Hollis, and the firm became the Cushman-Hollis Company.

The younger Cushman built on his father's experiments and began turning out a line of white canvas shoes and a type of athletic shoe. In fact, Auburn became known as "the White Shoe City of the World," Skinner wrote.

The white shoe fad peaked around 1917, he said. At that time, the company had twenty-one hundred employees who produced twenty-six thousand pairs of shoes every day.

Styles had reverted to more traditional shoes by the end of the First World War, a trend that meant a reduced role for the large Auburn firm. Nevertheless, Skinner said Auburn was fifth in national shoe output in 1922. Then the Great Depression hit and fortunes changed. A shoe strike in 1932 forced factory closures in Auburn, and Skinner reported lost payroll at $400,000.

Under a reorganization plan, Cushman operated until 1964 on a smaller scale.

Construction of the Union Street Bypass resulted in demolition of the great building, and the site is now occupied by a restaurant and part of the four-lane extension of Minot Avenue.

Those are the hard and cold facts, but many area residents may recall a view of the big brick building from the lunch counters of the old Mac's Variety Store on one street corner or Seavey's on the other corner.

There was a small retail shoe store in the building in its later years, and a friend once told me that Senator Margaret Chase Smith bought shoes there. My wife, Judy, had a high school job at Seavey's, and she remembers Senator Smith dropping in to purchase a newspaper.

So, you see, postcards can trigger all kinds of memories and emotions.

THE CORN FACTORY

For youngsters brought up on a farm, the fun factor of a cornfield rated high. Well, it wasn't all fun. First came planting the tar-coated kernels of corn that were meant to foil hungry crows. This practice always resulted in black, sticky and smelly fingers at the end of the day.

As the corn grew, there would be days of hoeing weeds in the hot sun, but eventually the corn would climb to heights just right for hide-and-seek games by preteen boys like my brother, Jim, and me. The cornfield became a jungle where leopards could pounce or a forest where Indians hid.

Near the end of August, my father and grandfather would search—stalk by stalk—for the best ears of corn to represent Echo Farm at the Maine State Fair. Those stalks were off-limits until fair week came and the Sugar and Gold sweet corn entries headed to the exhibition hall.

As the middle of September approached, it was time for the real harvest, when each ear was stripped by hand from the stalk and

Court Street, Auburn, looking toward the bridge, when horses, electric trolleys and automobiles shared the roadway. Auburn Hall (right) has been restored and is again the official town hall.

dropped in wire-handled bushel baskets. The baskets were dumped over the high sides of our Ford Model A truck until the mound topped the roof of the cab.

Truckload after truckload of corn rolled off the field and headed a couple of miles to the "corn factory." The factory, I recall, was located on Lake Auburn Avenue a short distance from my elementary school (the original two-story Washburn School with its distinctive bell tower). The Lake Auburn Towne House, built in 1968 as a one-hundred-unit housing facility for the elderly, now stands on the site of the old corn factory.

The large yard at the factory was dominated by a long, open-sided structure parallel to the street. Its roof stood high enough so that several trucks could back up under it on each side. The loads of corn would be raked off by hand onto a conveyor belt in the middle of the receiving area. The belt carried the corn into a large building, where employees husked the ears and prepared them for the canning process.

My memories stop at that conveyor belt. It was a fascinating operation for a young boy. I never saw what was inside the factory, but I'm sure there are many residents of the Twin Cities who recall working there.

Early Industry

In *Auburn 1869–1969: 100 Years a City*, Skinner filled out a lot of details about the local canning industry. United Packers put up the first factory in the 1880s, when Lake Auburn Avenue was called French Street. Later, "Burnham-Morrill took over the old horse car barn at 74 French Street and converted it into a canning factory," the book said, adding that the factory was destroyed by lightning. When it was rebuilt, the factory became "the largest and longest operating canning shop in Auburn." The last pack there was made in 1949.

"[Burnham-Morrill] did an extensive business and put out such products as baked beans," Skinner reports. "He specialized in custom canning. After he retired, the factory was demolished."

Other operations recorded in Skinner's book were a West Auburn canning business run by Philip Hiitt. That family business produced chicken pies and baked beans in the 1950s and 1960s. From 1941 to 1952, the Maine Baking Company on Minot Avenue also put out baked beans.

NORTH AUBURN CANNING FACTORY

Most supermarket carts reach the checkout counter these days loaded with dozens of canned products. We don't give a second thought to the process involved in producing that can of vegetables, fruit or berries, except for a vague assumption that it all takes place in some gigantic facility far away.

That wasn't always the case. At one time, many local families had gardens where they would plant, nurture and harvest a variety of crops meant to provide meals for several coming months. Several methods of home food preservation were used then, as now, but it's not widely remembered that local canning factories could take on small orders for families, as well as the contract jobs for large farms.

The North Auburn Canning Factory located at Church Corner was one such operation. The canning season began in July with cherries and peaked in August when tons of beans were being picked. It continued through the sweet corn and tomato season into the early fall for squash and pumpkins.

An August 1945 issue of the *Lewiston Evening Journal* magazine section profiled the factory in a piece written by Ina N. McCausland. She captured some descriptions of a unique period of industrialization that mixed business with democracy at a truly neighborhood level.

McCausland told how James Webster Bennett—known as Webb to his friends and employees—acquired the old Lakeside Packing Company at Little Wilson Pond in 1911. It was moved to North Auburn in 1919, and for several decades, Bennett ran a modest commercial and custom canning operation.

It was the informality of the business that intrigued McCausland. She described a typical day when members of nearly every family in North Auburn and Dillingham Hill would gather for work at the cannery. Women showed up with their favorite knives, a few men who were not involved in summer farm work would come to the factory to augment their incomes and some youngsters also pitched in. A job in the cannery was also a social event. The neighbors swapped local news and gossip as they went about their tasks.

Under the supervision of Bennett and his wife, the workers would look at the day's orders and divide up the duties. Beans were the principal crop every summer, and the first order of business was snipping off the ends of each pod by hand. Next, the beans went into wire baskets for blanching—a quick dip in scalding water. Tin cans were arrayed at the filling table to receive the hot beans and a cover was dropped onto the top of each can and sealed in place.

The cooking took place in the retort, which most people would call the pressure cooker. When the cooking was complete, large batches of hot cans were lifted out by block and table, and they dried by evaporation under their own heat. There was a small hole in each cover, and the final step was to solder this shut. Lot numbers were printed on the cans to match up with the crop's owner, and labels were applied.

Beans came in from large Maine farms near and far. Every can was processed and marked so that each farmer got only his own crop back when he returned and loaded hundreds of cans at the end of the day.

The small custom orders were scheduled for days between the major jobs. A family in a nearby town would write to Bennett and arrange a schedule for the canning of their harvest. Then, on the morning of a set date, they would drop off the garden produce and head off for a day of shopping in Lewiston. Later in the day, they would return to North Auburn to pick up the cans that would provide homegrown food for months to come.

It's told that Mrs. Bennett's four-year-old nephew was helping pack cans one day on the cooking pan. At noon, she decided to encourage the boy, so she gave him three shiny fifty-cent pieces. He clutched them in his hand and started to leave.

"Where are you going?" his surprised aunt asked.

"I'm going home," he said. "I've got enough money."

EARLY PAPERMAKERS

Papermaking has a long history in the Pine Tree State, but that industry had only a small presence in the L-A area. Most papermaking was connected with the large forests of Maine and the all-important wood fiber they supplied.

That wasn't always the case. Paper was once a product of other fibers mostly found in rags. In Westbrook, Maine, adjacent to Portland, the early S.D. Warren Paper Mill received big shipments of cotton mummy wrappings from Egypt for conversion into paper.

A couple of mills on the Little Androscoggin River in Mechanic Falls played a major role in the paper industry around the time of the transition from rag to wood fiber. Tons of rags arrived at the Eagle Mill Paper Works for transformation into paper in the 1850s. Descriptions of the process were printed in a December 3, 1858 issue of the *Lewiston Falls Journal* and reprinted in the 1993 commemoratory history of Mechanic Falls from files of the Androscoggin Historical Society.

The three-story Eagle Mill was described as "substantial, commodious and convenient," and it was built on seventeen hundred cubic feet of solid granite basement walls. The newspaper noted, "All the heavy machinery now moves with scarcely a perceptible jar."

It's the description of the papermaking process that is particularly fascinating. Most of the fiber stock came from the cotton and other mills in Lewiston and other communities. Old sails and rope from thousands of Maine vessels also supplied much of the hundreds of tons used yearly. Trimmings from government documents in Washington, D.C., were baled and delivered to the Maine mill. Lastly, many "rag pickers" collected cloth that amounted to ten or twenty tons annually.

The newspaper continued:

> *The principal collectors of the latter are the tin peddlers who are constantly scouring the country, getting a few pounds at this house and a few pounds at that. As but a few of these itinerant merchants trade directly with the paper mill, they dispose of their rag accumulations at some general rag depot which happens to be in their particular "beat" of the country.*

The rag pickers got three to six cents a pound for domestic rags, while the cotton waste from area mills brought two to seven cents a pound.

The first step in extracting tiny fibers was a trip through a four-sided revolving wire cylinder called an "elephant duster." There also was a "threshing and deviling duster" for coarser stock such as ropes and bagging.

The partly cleaned rags went next to a sorting room on an upper floor, where about a dozen young women were employed to divide the stock by quality and color.

From this point on, the process was much like today's papermaking from wood pulp. After bleaching, the stock was reduced to a milky solution by beaters, and it became paper on a moving endless wire mesh, where water drained out, and the new paper moved through rollers across heated cylinders.

The account noted, "Two men only are required to superintend the operation of the 'Machine,' while three girls look after the paper" as it came off.

Another historically significant paper mill operated in Mechanic Falls. A mill that came to be known as Dennison Paper Manufacturing Company was built on the Little Androscoggin in 1865. Its place in history comes from its experimentation with the chemical process of reducing wood to pulp for paper.

Poole's 1890 History of Poland says, "We believe this company was the first to make paper exclusively of all wood, which they did for a long time previous to 1887."

PART II

Snow, Flood and Fire

NICE SLEIGHING

Today, we wonder how people ever got around before roads were paved, especially in wintertime in the days before roads were plowed, sanded and salted—and they often did it day and night in horse-drawn carriages through blowing snow.

As I read the pages of my great-grandmother's diary from the winter of 1896, I realized that all of this was taken for granted. In fact, most people felt they were traveling in the most up-to-date fashion. In town, there were several livery stables, including the R.S. Bradbury Stable at the Auburn end of the bridge. There were horse-drawn trolleys that were replaced by electric cars near the end of the century.

We now want our roads cleared immediately after snowstorms, but it was almost the opposite a century ago. A good base of packed snow on the road meant good sledding, and the daily diary entries of Dorcas Field emphasized the importance of those conditions.

On November 21, 1896, she wrote, "Snowing hard." And the next day, she said, "Ern [her brother Ernest, who ran a milk route] went on runners today. I went to church in the sleigh. It was nice sleighing."

My granddaughter
Heather Fellman models
a fancy gown of heavy
material that was probably
worn by my great-
grandmother after the
Civil War.

And then a thaw came, and she spoke of putting the wheels back on the carriage. As the winter season progressed, the desire was for consistent cold and sufficient snow. In mid-January, she wrote that two inches of snow fell, but "not enough to do any good, as the wind blew it all off."

In another entry, she mentioned a winter sleigh ride to a grange meeting fifteen miles away in South Paris. The next day, she said she felt "a bit sore from the ride."

The most remarkable fact to me as I read this diary was the frequency of winter trips to town, to friends' houses and to meetings. My great-grandmother mentioned all kinds of jaunts by family members several times a week. Nothing seemed to stop them. They called it "gallivanting."

Our old family diaries provide me with a rich resource of daily observation from the late 1800s. My great-grandparents viewed the weather of their day from a different perspective. A frozen river was necessary to ensure a good ice harvest. It also meant that quite a few miles could be saved when the family hitched the horse to the sleigh for a trip to visit relatives in Greene. Our farm is on the Auburn side of the river, so the ability to go upstream and cross the frozen river was much better than traveling downstream to cross the bridge at Court Street.

In the days before Gulf Island Dam was constructed and put into service in the 1920s, the Androscoggin River had a more consistent flow. Ice formed early in the winter, and it easily reached thicknesses of sixteen to twenty inches. That's what was needed for cutting and storing blocks in the farm's icehouse for use through the coming summer.

My great-grandmother's diary of 1896 had several references to the river ice. On January 5, she wrote, "Pleasant but very cold. No snow yet. River frozen over, very rough, all anchor ice."

Five days later, she said, "Charlie Waterman came over to break a road [across the riverside fields] to haul wood across the river."

On January 15, she told about the men of the family helping a neighbor with the first ice cutting of the season.

"They finished filling the ice house," she noted on February 20. Then she wrote about the men helping neighbors with their ice harvests. The tasks of cutting ice and "working up" firewood filled just about every winter day, but she also wrote often about visits to friends and relatives

My father, Walter Sargent, "works up" wood for the furnace and stoves. This was a routine job on the farm, as were dairy barn and garden chores.

and trips to town for photograph sessions, drama club meetings and shows—and they seldom missed a Grange meeting.

I can't help wondering where future generations will read about the daily lives and observations of the present. There's very little letter writing these days. People talk on the phone; they send e-mail and text messages and even briefer "Twitter" notes. There's very little personal written record.

It may not be entries by pen in a diary, but my wife, Judy, keeps a journal on her computer. It chronicles her daily routine of flower gardening, sightings of birds and animals around the farm and notes on local activity. When there's significant national or world news, she will comment on those events and what people may be saying.

That's what diaries once gave us. After reading so many fascinating passages in our ancestors' diaries, Judy has a keen appreciation for the importance of her own journal to those who will come later.

WINTERS...AND POLLY THE HORSE

Winters aren't like they used to be. Any old-timer will tell you that.

About fifty years ago, the snow would drift halfway up the windows on the west side of the farmhouse. Sometimes we waited and watched for two days for the plows to break our road open.

I remember those winters well. At least, I think I do, but nothing magnifies memories about the severity of weather like the passage of time.

Stories about the old-time winters fascinate me, and I learned a little more about those times in an article written by a Turner teacher in 1922. Sarah Hopkins wrote in the *Lewiston Journal* about the winter of 1872, when she taught at the North Parish School. She recalled a visit to a student's home in the northern part of the town.

"I remember the drifts eight feet deep through which we rode, perhaps three feet over our heads, on the way back to school," she said.

When she talked about those days, her opinions were not so different from what you might hear today: "Sixty years ago no one ever came to take the children to school every day and to transport them in autos and teams to their homes."

In the mid-1800s, farmers took great pride in their matched yokes of oxen. Sarah Hopkins described how they used the teams to break open the roads, "calling it fun to shovel through the great drifts of snow for which Turner is famous."

"Today," she continued, "the boys esteem it a hard job and wait for the winds to stop blowing before hitching the work horses to the roller to break the roads."

This teacher had an admiring recollection of one Turner resident, probably one of her students.

"I have seen Win Allen of Chase's Mills sit down in the road in the snow, take his boots off, and rub his feet, they were so cold, to keep them from freezing, put on his boots, say nothing and pursue his onward way," she wrote.

Nothing was said in Sarah Hopkins's accounts about snow days, storms so bad that school was called off.

She recalled the times when she was a young girl and some assistance was offered on the worst winter days.

"Marcus Sampson might be depended upon to take us youngsters home on the ox sled after a big storm," she said.

Whether they are tales of long ago or as recent as the great ice storm of 1998, every family in a northern latitude will have remarkable winter stories to tell.

My father published a small book of poems and prose in 1983 called *Homespun*. In it, he recalls a January thaw in 1928, when my grandfather hitched Old Polly—"the meanest mare that ever lived"—to a sleigh and headed to town for a load of grain.

Old Polly was tough to manage and had a tendency to bite.

"One day, Pa stooped. She grabbed him by the belt. He carried teeth marks on his back to his grave."

Nevertheless, Dad says my grandfather forgave everything after that winter day when he claimed Old Polly saved his life.

"The weather turned to a snarlin' blizzard—blotted everything," my father wrote. The sleigh sank and stuck in the rain-softened snow on the road, and my grandfather fumbled in the swirling snow to unhook the trace chains.

"Pa gave the mare her head and hung to a britchin' strap," the story said. His wet clothes froze, as did his eyes and hair. Polly's, too, crusted over.

"When I opened the big barn door, I scarcely knew the pair," my father wrote.

Depression and the Flood of 1936

In the decade following the October 24, 1929 stock market crash, Maine citizens battled the consequences of unemployment and lost dreams. Mainers were coping with the Great Depression in March 1936. Did the newspaper reflect despair? Were people overwhelmed and defeated? You wouldn't know it. After all, it's Maine, where people know how to "make do."

They were mostly working hard, watching their pennies and doing quite well. The ads featured washing machines and furniture. Peck's sold imported handmade linens for one dollar, and Kresge's advertised housedresses for a dollar. L-A residents were flocking to the Shrine Circus at the Lewiston Armory. The popular orchestra of Lloyd Rafnell was to play at Auburn Hall—admission ten cents. The Empire Theatre was showing a documentary about the Dionne Quintuplets. Those five baby girls born almost two years earlier were the subjects of tremendous national curiosity.

Nevertheless, it was the eve of an event that would turn the world upside down again. Temperatures were warm, and it was raining that week. It was raining a lot.

On March 9, a warm, moisture-laden front moved into and stalled over New England, resulting in unseasonably warm temperatures and heavy rainfall. Totals topped fifteen inches of rain in a fourteen-day period. A deep snow pack melted rapidly, and rivers that had been choked with ice overflowed their banks. The *Lewiston Daily Sun* headlined: "Floods Grip All Western Maine."

The Androscoggin River was among the waterways where damage was most severe, and many riverside areas of L-A were impacted. At Gulf Island Dam, the river roared over at 212,000 cubic feet per second, topping the previous record of 60,000.

More than a dozen railroad cars filled with gravel were pulled onto the trestle spanning Great Falls. The extra weight was meant to keep the bridge from washing away.

Floodwaters pound North Bridge at the height of the Androscoggin River flood of 1936, but the bridge held. *Courtesy the* Lewiston Sun Journal.

Part of South Bridge, now named the Lown Peace Bridge, was washed away, and massive blocks of ice and debris battered North Bridge (Longley Memorial Bridge), but it stood solid.

In New Auburn, the raging Little Androscoggin toppled houses on Newbury Street. In Lewiston, water isolated large sections around Oxford Street, known as Little Canada, and a stream at Crowley's Junction flooded a large area.

Rumford and nearby towns also experienced devastation from the flooding. A newspaper headline read, "Lewiston Sends Special Train with Dynamite for Rumford Ice Jams." Many men risked their lives to set explosives and push the floating ice and debris along. Some threatening pieces of ice were said to be larger than a football field.

All motor routes into the Twin Cities were cut off by the high water, and a North Jay man was killed when an avalanche swept a shed into a brook.

The aftermath of that 1936 flood was felt for years, and its devastation was unequalled, although another major flood in 1987 came close.

Snow, Flood and Fire

These buildings at a lumberyard in Lewiston were among the many riverside structures destroyed in the Androscoggin River flood of 1936. *Courtesy the* Lewiston Sun Journal.

The Great Depression hit Maine people hard, but they managed to get through it. As often happens when things seem to be going better, something unexpected comes along to upset it all. Years of economic struggle can test the resolve of the population, but Mother Nature likes to remind us from time to time that she can always throw us some complications.

Bridge Out!

Crossing the Androscoggin River between Auburn and Lewiston is a pretty routine matter these days. It's a short drive across one of four principal bridges, and there's not much time to take in the view, except for a glance at the Great Falls.

Years ago, the linking of the east and west shores of the Androscoggin by bridge was a very important accomplishment. North Bridge, now

The Androscoggin River rages in the flood of 1896.

known as the James B. Longley Memorial Bridge, has been a solid and reliable connector for many years, but it was preceded by wooden bridges that were much more vulnerable to nature's extremes.

The bridge between Auburn's Court Street and Lewiston's Main Street served well for many decades in the 1800s. It was a toll bridge in its early history. I have a toll ticket from the days when my great-grandparents and their family used it regularly. The early spring freshet of 1896 washed that wooden structure away, and as I learned from the diary of my great-grandmother, that loss led to considerable hardship and danger.

Dorcas Field wrote about the trials and tribulations of her brother, Ernest, as he tried to maintain his milk delivery route.

"Ern carried milk across the railroad bridge," the diary reports on March 3, the day after the calamity. "He got home at three o'clock. Oh, it is a wild, frightening sight."

With no bridge, the only other way to cross the river was by ferry, which local people set up within a few days.

Dorcas wrote, "Ern carried his horse over the river and left him and hauled his milk over in the wagon."

I often wondered how a ferry could ever be employed to cross a rushing river that had destroyed a bridge. The answer for me was in a description of a ferry's operation on the Androscoggin at West Bethel.

Frank Worcester, writing in a June 1979 issue of the *Bethel Courier*, said that a large steel cable attached to two double poles on each side of the river was the means employed at a site in his town. On the ferryman's home side, the cable could be loosened or tightened on a windlass (a simple winch) to adjust for the rise and fall of the river.

It might be imagined that the ferry moved across by pulling a rope. This was not so. It was much more ingenious than that.

A heavy rope on each end of the flatboat went to a two-wheel cable trolley. A rope crank on the rail made it possible for the ferryman to adjust the ferry's angle to the cable.

The river's current was the means of propulsion. Borrowing from the principles of wind on the angled sails of a schooner, the moving water pushed against the side of the boat and against two heavy sideboards that could be levered down when water depth allowed. The angle to the current squeezed the ferry through the water.

As if the 1896 flood were not enough, the coming week in March brought "the heaviest snow storm we have had all winter." That was good fortune, though, and Dorcas noted "fine sleighing" for several days.

The lack of a bridge affected Lewiston-Auburn residents throughout the year. It was December before a new North Bridge was opened. Its cost was about $146,000, and two-thirds of that was borne by Lewiston. The six-hundred-foot all-steel plate girder structure rested on six granite piers and two abutments.

The *Lewiston Journal* reported that a Lewiston official, Alderman Wiggin, "stepped forth from the small crowd of dignitaries, and with an ax he proceeded to smash down the bars." That led to an impromptu footrace from Auburn to the Lewiston end between a committee member, O.W. Jones, and a local citizen, Frank A. Chase. Jones won.

Lewiston mayor Frank L. Noble said, "I see no reason for speech making. It's a good bridge and we're proud of it."

There are many other sights that can no longer be seen when crossing the river these days.

If the Veterans Memorial Bridge that leads to the Auburn Mall area had existed more than one hundred years ago, winter commuters would have seen a spectacular toboggan run on the Lewiston shore just north of Boxer Island. It began at the top of a fairly large hill and went right to the shore, where toboggans could shoot onto the ice for an extra-long ride.

Crossing the Androscoggin has taken many forms, from bridges to ferries to ice. There were times you could walk across—not on the river bottom but on floating logs.

The Androscoggin is not often thought of as a river on which huge log drives took place, but they happened here, and on a grand scale. There were several weeks of the year after a winter of cutting in forestland to the north that thousands of logs were floated downstream to sawmills. A stretch of river above the Great Falls was an important holding area for the logs. That was before the 1902 construction of the Libbey-Dingley Dam, now called Deer Rips Dam, and Gulf Island Dam in the mid-1920s.

Two large piles of rocks enclosed by a square of log cribbing can be seen below Deer Rips and just offshore from my family's fields. When the dams occasionally hold water back and levels drop very low, nearly two dozen other rock piers can be seen in the channel.

There's a large boulder on our family's riverfront shore. A huge iron ring is attached to it. Chains were run from that ring to piers, and various log companies had their pens to hold logs until sawmills were ready to receive them. Each pen's logs were branded with the owner's mark.

Today, we whiz across this great river with barely a look at it. Those who are now working for its restoration and recreation potential are rediscovering its value, both historical and future.

BRIDGES OF ALL KINDS

Rivers need bridges. Not just the concrete, wood or steel variety but also connectors for community. You'll see a lot of that kind of connectivity on the Fourth of July, when hundreds of families gather on or near the Governor James B. Longley Memorial Bridge, their "ooohhs" and "aaahhs" rising and falling in verbal accompaniment to bursts of color over the Great Falls. Lewiston-Auburn's Liberty Festival is a prime example of the bridge-for-community metaphor.

Looking at the area's physical bridges, it's easy to see diversity of structure, purpose and historical uses. In the earliest days of L-A's development, there were sites where ferries moved people and their goods across the Androscoggin River. Ferry Road in Lewiston near Lisbon is a present-day reminder of that time.

Winter ice or bad weather put limits on ferry use, so construction of bridges became a priority. The first bridge between the evolving downtown areas of the towns was made of wood, and it was originally a toll bridge.

Through the years, that bridge near the falls has seen much reconstruction and many changes, including its name. For older

My great-grandmother's family used this pass when a wooden toll bridge connected Auburn and Lewiston.

generations, it was always North Bridge. I remember when high board windbreaks were erected just before winter each year to protect walkers from the bitterly cold blasts off the falls.

Though early spans were washed away in floods, the current level on concrete piers survives the frequent high water and provides some spectacular views when the river rages.

In the great flood of 1936, South Bridge between New Auburn and Lewiston's "Little Canada" was partially swept away. It was rebuilt in its present steel truss form.

The river's fury severely tested the Twin Cities' bridges in 1936, but just a year later there was even more turbulence, and this time it was on the top side of the northern span. Many L-A neighbors found themselves pitted against one another in fear and anger as a long and sometimes violent strike by shoe workers in nineteen factories, mostly in Auburn, spilled across the river. Nearly sixty-five hundred people were thrown out of work. The ninety-six-day strike received national news attention. Six factories never reopened.

Local police were forced into raising their clubs against residents, including women, who were divided in their loyalties to family, community, employers and co-workers.

My mother, Lona Sargent, was among those affected workers. It was a couple of years before I was born, and she was working in a local shoe shop to supplement the farm income.

We heard stories of how she quietly and resolutely crossed the picket lines, not in defiance of organization efforts or labor causes the other workers may have felt they needed to support, but because she felt simply that she had a job, she had a right to do it and she would go ahead and do what she had to do for her family.

From March 1937 into the summer, it was a very difficult period in L-A's history. The Maine National Guard was called out for seventeen days to keep order. Simply crossing that bridge in those days must have taken considerable courage and determination. Emotional scars of that strike remained for years, as they do in all communities where ethnic or economic issues divide the populace.

The Grand Trunk Railroad once had a passenger station in Auburn near Court Street. Most Franco-American families arriving from Canada traveled a mile farther to the Lewiston station.

A few years ago, South Bridge was renamed the Bernard Lown Peace Bridge in honor of the Lewiston native and Nobel Peace Prize recipient. He is a world-renowned cardiologist and peace activist.

Railroads are the reason for a couple of other local bridges. The span known as the Maine Central Railroad trestle above the falls still carries dozens of freight cars across each day.

Downriver, the old Grand Trunk Railroad Bridge is now a pedestrian walkway between Auburn's Bonney Park and Lewiston's Simard-Payne Memorial Park.

Near here generations ago, thousands of French-Canadian families completed their immigration to our cities, and now the community linkage has evolved literally from mass transportation to individual and personal use by L-A's citizens.

While we drive and walk across these river bridges, including the Maine Turnpike Bridge built in the mid-1950s and a few others across the canals and the Little Androscoggin in New Auburn, we should note the many other bridges being formed between cultures, such as the impressive Africana Festival and Somali celebrations. Even our municipal governments are exploring ways of bridging the two cities' purchases and services.

There are many kinds of bridges that can bring us all together.

BUILDING GULF ISLAND DAM

"It will never be the same" is a mantra that accompanies change everywhere, and it is usually uttered with an unnecessary sense of despair. But just look around—things everywhere are not the same. Our part of the Androscoggin Valley has undergone drastic change since the early days of Auburn and Lewiston, and for the most part, we have reaped great benefits.

Most L-A residents know about the Gulf Island Dam, a major hydroelectric facility a few miles upstream from the cities' bridges. Very few have actually seen it because roads don't pass directly within sight of it. Fewer still know its history.

Gulf Island Dam is probably the single greatest agent of change in our region's history and the best example of the mirror meanings of "it will never be the same."

I'm preserving a small collection of Gulf Island Dam construction photos taken by my father in the summer of 1926, when he was fifteen years old. There's also material from the writings of my aunt, Edith Labbie, that appeared in the *Lewiston Evening Journal*.

All of this documents a massive project that employed a small army of laborers who lived in on-site barracks. Calvin Irish and his wife had a front-yard view of the project from their Auburn farm, knowing that much of the farm's two hundred acres would soon disappear under the water the dam would capture. Nevertheless, that farm supplied fresh milk, eggs, vegetables and drinking water for the men in the new bunkhouse.

In the early 1920s, farmers along the river heard about plans for a power plant. Surveyors scouted riverbank land, and deals were made to buy up farms that would soon become flooded. Easements were secured for pole lines along the shore, including along my family's farm fields.

Construction on the $5 million project was moving into high gear for the summer of 1926. The curved structure was eventually going to measure twenty-two hundred feet across the river. That's almost half a mile. It would rise to fifty-eight feet with a sixty-foot base tapering upward to sixteen feet wide at the top. Work would be finished in the following year.

A cofferdam was an early step in the construction of Gulf Island Dam in 1926–27. The concrete structure spans nearly half a mile.

Drill crews spent months boring test holes for the dam's foundation. Four cofferdams were the first step in construction, diverting the river around the work areas so fill could be dumped and immense concrete forms erected on a steel skeleton.

On the Lewiston side, a spur railroad was built to bring gravel from Leeds to the Switzerland Road. The concrete made from it traveled out above the river on large cable cars to be dumped into the forms.

Hundreds of men worked two shifts of twelve hours each. In the early stages, they had to walk a high, swaying suspension bridge, lighted at night, to get from one side to the other. My aunt remembered walking the bridge when she was only seven years old.

Flooding the land to create Gulf Island Pond began on September 20, 1926. It took forty-three days for the water level to rise from 8.7 feet to 48.7 feet.

Today, we can sit on the riverbank of our woodlot and enjoy a spectacular view of Gulf Island Dam. Its construction had a tremendous psychological effect on shore-land owners, but over the years my family reaped unforeseen benefits from this great alteration of the Androscoggin. The North River Road was once a busy dirt road that took people past our 150-year-old farm between Auburn and Turner. The dam meant that all kinds of development took place along Center Street, and our road became a relatively quiet country byway.

Upstream paper mills were principal causes of pollution in the Androscoggin River, and though it's greatly improved today, there's still room for water-quality improvement.

I often feel I am hearing too many calls for an immediate remedy, as well as too many news reports and analysis that still talk about the Androscoggin as the "most polluted" river in the nation. History tells us that this is a river of many changes—good, bad, fast and slow—and I hope any new changes proceed with realistic expectations.

LISBON'S PAINT MINE

Chances are you have never heard of a paint mine. And you might also be surprised to learn that Lisbon, just south of Lewiston, had its own paint mine a little more than one hundred years ago. Local people worked at a downtown factory beside the railroad tracks at the corner of what's now called Winter Street.

Down through history—even as early as cave drawings—people have used paint, and the earth itself has been the source of its color and substance. Nevertheless, we seldom realize in this day and age that it wasn't so long ago that the basis for a local paint-making business could be found right beneath our feet.

The enterprise began in 1885 as the New England Mineral Paint Co. and was restructured after its first couple of years into the Lisbon Paint Company. Its operations were out of a newly built wooden building with a flat roof. It was said to have grinders and mixing machines powered by huge boilers.

According to an account by Richard Plante in the *Lewiston Evening Journal* about sixty years ago, the actual mineral paint material was found on land about half a mile away. The mining process was basic: scoop the mineral pigment off the surface of the land and load it by hand onto horse-drawn wagons. Plante said the operation covered a major expanse in those days, but very little sign of it remained a couple of decades later.

The mineral deposit needed for the making of paint was discovered on property owned by Edward N. Chamberland, a farmer and maker of wooden consumer products, when some timber was being cut on his land. Chamberland sent a sample off for testing. A *Lewiston Evening Journal* story on September 21, 1884, said, "A barrel of paint from Chamberland's paint mine in Lisbon has been ground up by a Massachusetts paint firm and found highly satisfactory. It is being tested for permanency of color."

The Lisbon firm turned out cans of paint for shipment throughout the region, but it was not a great success. Metal pigments for making paint were coming into common use, and manufacturers were turning away from mineral paint deposits. The Lisbon Paint Company came to an untimely end in July 1889, when fire leveled the factory.

Sensational Shiloh at Durham

What's going on there? What are they hiding? They're not like us. It must be something terrible.

That kind of sentiment could come right out of today's headlines. Actually, it's the kind of thing people in this area were saying one hundred years ago about the sprawling complex of buildings at the Shiloh Colony in Durham, just south of Auburn. A gigantic temple topped the hill overlooking the Androscoggin River, and several other large buildings became part of the religious community founded by Frank W. Sandford, a controversial leader of the prophetic Christian movement known as the Kingdom. The meteoric rise in converts who flocked to Shiloh led to much ill-informed opposition and distrust.

Farmers sold their land and brought their families to Shiloh. Generous gifts of money flowed in, and at its peak, Shiloh had six hundred permanent residents devoted to Bible study and a ritual of twenty-four-hour prayer. Some fifty years ago, the largest of the empty buildings was dismantled. Some smaller ones, including a chapel, remain today.

What made this evangelical movement and its spectacular presence in rural Maine so controversial? Sandford's charismatic personality drew totally dedicated followers, but a string of tragic circumstances ensued. Sandford wanted to take the movement worldwide. He took a few dozen Shilohites on a schooner to stops in Africa and elsewhere in 1911. Eventually, a series of errors left the ship under-supplied. Some people died, and charges were brought against Sandford. He refused to defend himself and was sentenced to serve time at an Atlanta prison. By the 1930s, the Kingdom's subjects were becoming scattered.

The facts about Shiloh, and a lot of sensationalism, can be found in great detail in many books and on the Internet. It's all fascinating, but there is one published summary of life at Shiloh that is a good starting point to understanding life in that enigmatic Durham enclave.

Reverend Frank S. Murray, Sandford's biographer and disciple, told about life at Shiloh at a 1967 meeting of the Androscoggin County Historical Society covered by Mildred Cole of the *Lewiston Daily Sun*.

Her account of the lecture said:

> *The first building was the central edifice with the towers. It was called Shiloh, a word meaning tranquil or restful. Six Bible School students and Mr. Sandford started the structure in 1896 with only one cent in cash and a borrowed wheelbarrow.*
>
> *In 1897, a temple was built in Auburn at the corner of Summer and Union Streets. It remained there until 1904, when it was moved to Durham, and re-erected on a different plan.*

Shiloh's first chapel held three hundred people, but the temple built soon after could accommodate seven hundred. Cole's story continued:

> *The central structure was crowned with a seven-story turret in which perpetual prayers were said, both night and day for 23 years. As soon as Shiloh proper was completed, it was too small*

The massive temple of Shiloh, a religious community plagued by controversy, stood on a hill at Durham, near Auburn.

to accommodate the membership, so they had to start building the extension. It was a huge structure described as roughly comparable to the Poland Spring House.

In addition to the central structure, Shiloh owned some twenty-two farms in Durham, with an acreage amounting to about two square miles.

Murray lived at Shiloh until he was about ten years old, when the community was disbanded in 1920. He attended school there and praised the system, Cole said.

Murray's lecture described the daily routine. He said the night watchman would light the boilers at 3:00 a.m. At 4:00 a.m., he would awaken the cooks, and the rising bell for all rang at 6:00 a.m. After an hour of private devotions, breakfast (the first of two daily meals at Shiloh) was at 8:00 a.m. At 9:00 a.m. there was a meeting in the chapel, during which forty minutes were spent on the knees praying.

According to Cole's account:

Bible School commenced at 10:30 a.m. and would go on indefinitely, sometimes running through the entire day and into the night. However,

it usually ended about 2 or 2:30 p.m. The supper hour was at 4 p.m.,
followed by an evening meeting, and lights out at 10 p.m. Murray said
that Shiloh involved deeply religious work, with nothing bizarre or
outlandish about it.

Having weathered a painful past, small elements of the movement founded by Sandford, or variations thereof, continue with optimism at a half-dozen locations in the country, including Lisbon, where Murray's son has been the pastor.

Up in Flames

Whenever history goes up in flames, the loss is felt deeply and differently throughout a community.

The Cowen Mill conflagration on July 15, 2009, kindled many local memories. A few years earlier, fire had destroyed the adjoining Libbey Mill, and both of the familiar massive brick structures on the Lewiston side of the Androscoggin River's Great Falls have disappeared. Although the buildings were empty and unused in their final years, there were many local residents who spent their working lives in these big brick mills.

It was a similar quiet July day in 1987 when a fire alarm sounded at the Worumbo Mill in Lisbon Falls. A workman's blowtorch had sparked a small fire, but that's all it took to set off a conflagration that is still listed among the biggest fires in Maine's history.

When a major fire hits a small town, the effects are devastating. Fortunately, there was no loss of life or serious injury when the historic mill burned. Its heyday of manufacturing prized woolen goods was past, but many residents of the town had worked there, and its loss was a terrible blow that is still deeply felt.

The fire raged for more than two hours on that Thursday afternoon, and this time heroic efforts by about three hundred firefighters and many volunteers saved the local businesses from smoldering embers that fell everywhere.

Not long after the fire, Ambra Watkins wrote a small book called *The Birth, Being and Burning of Worumbo Mill.*

It was Otto Stewich, overseer of spinning and carding for thirty-seven years, who told her that the Worumbo "was just like one big happy family, by gosh."

"They all had a deep sense of pride in their work despite position," he told Watkins.

The workers had good reason to be proud. They produced fine fabrics from all kinds of animal hair: mohair, camel hair, chinchilla and fine wool from Austria and New Zealand. One exceptional product was made from the valuable hair of the vicuna, a South American animal that closely resembles a llama.

In her book, Watkins said that vicuna fiber was strictly regulated, and only a little more than a ton was shipped to this country each year. Most of that went to the Worumbo Mill.

Frank Conley was overseer of raw stock in the mill's trucking department for about forty-four years. He told Watkins how they would receive the material in a ball, which he would carefully weigh and run through a wire cylinder called a duster. Conley then had to gather all the fibers that fell on the floor and weigh them to determine the loss.

Vicuna cloth sold for $60 a yard, and a full coat of the material sold for $1,200. It was the kind of fashion prized by stars like Cary Grant and Wallace Beery, Watkins wrote. She also noted a national scandal in which a coat that could have contained cloth made in Lisbon Falls led to the downfall of Sherman Adams, a New Hampshire governor who became President Eisenhower's chief of staff. Adams had accepted the gift of a vicuna coat from a prominent Washington lobbyist.

Vicuna was also an excellent material for uniforms, including the deep indigo jackets of the New York City Police Department. The young ladies who worked with the indigo dye would come home sporting a blue hue on hot summer days.

The Worumbo Mill also used vicuna to produce "blizzard cloth," from which outerwear was made for Admiral Byrd's explorations of the Antarctic.

When the mill burned on that July day in 1987, vivid memories flashed through the minds of dozens of former workers who stood and watched. Some relived the stories of the acclaimed Worumbo Indians, a semipro baseball team that gained national stature. Worumbo's owners recruited top players to come to work at the mill and play on the team. They included Joe Kinney and Tony Begos, a talented shortstop who had played on an all-star team with Babe Ruth against Lou Gehrig. Begos also played in games against Jim Thorpe and Babe Didrickson. The most well-known Worumbo Indian was probably first baseman Eddie Waitkus, who went on to play with the Chicago Cubs and Philadelphia Phillies.

Fires may destroy massive mills and other workplaces, but those places remain alive in the memories of many people whose lives were shaped by their years inside those walls.

Lyceum Hall

Midway through the Victorian era, in September 1871, an important building designed by Lewiston architect Charles F. Douglas opened at 49 Lisbon Street. Lyceum Hall housed a grand theatre on the upper floors and new retail establishments on street level.

It was the city's first major theatrical venue. The public entered and ascended a wide staircase to the second floor, where a few professional offices lined the left side of a corridor and the theatre's reception and ticketing area was on the right. Another wide staircase at the back went to the wide-open third and fourth floors, with seating for one thousand on the main level and on a large mezzanine. The stage was built along the Lisbon Street side of the hall.

It's now only a shell of its former grandeur. Once, celebrities like Buffalo Bill and Wild Bill Hickok appeared there, but remnants of wainscoted walls and ornate banisters can still be seen. Overhead, there are two massive heat chimneys, which are inverted funnel-shaped structures with ceiling openings about ten feet square. On summer days, those chimneys exhausted excess heat.

The remains of this old theatre are fascinating to see today, but it's the activity on the ground floor that really ignites my imagination. The upscale

A view of Lisbon Street around 1900, looking north to the "head of the street" and the Great Department Store, later the popular Peck's store.

Fuel Restaurant enjoyed a highly successful opening year in 2007 under owners Eric and Carrie Agren, and next door, Gallery 5 of L/A Arts complements the cuisine with a chance to view and buy works by area artists.

Eric Agren showed me his Lyceum Hall, top to bottom, and talked about his passion for saving all the best of the old. He and his wife live above the restaurant-gallery space in a remarkable renovation of the space below the old theatre. They kept brick walls, beams and even a door in their modern kitchen with faint lettering: "Ladies Toilet."

As we walked the dark and empty upper floor, Eric pointed out old woodwork of the original theatre that he and his wife utilized to make their dining table.

Eric explained to me that the original owners of the large new structure were Richards and Merrill, and they had a men's clothing store where the restaurant is now located. On the Gallery 5 side was Owens and Little, a hardware store that was a predecessor of Hall and Knight Hardware, a well-known Lewiston business for many years. Other retail space in Lyceum Hall was occupied by Berry Paper Co. in the 1920s through the 1950s or '60s, and it also housed Ilona's Hairstyling and office space for Androscoggin Bank.

PART III

People and Recreation

Vinegar Inspector and Culler of Staves

You won't find many inspectors of vinegar on the governmental payrolls of Lewiston and Auburn these days. There aren't many fence viewers or cullers of staves or tythingmen, either.

I didn't expect to find so many similarities with today's headlines or home life when I started looking at some 125-year-old copies of Lewiston and Auburn annual reports. That was a period when my great-grandfather, David P. Field, served as an Auburn alderman, and I hoped to learn more about our family's history.

As I thumbed through the annual reports' pages, I found passage after passage that suggested a modern parallel.

W.A. Robinson, Auburn's inspector of vinegar in 1883, reported that the thirteen samples he tested revealed adulteration in three of them, two with sulfuric acid and one with muriatic acid.

The quality of vinegar had major importance in those days. Laws required that it be of pure apple origin, and attempts to "tone up" the acidity by chemical additions were illegal. In fact, the vinegar inspector had precise rules for measuring and testing using the latest science of the day. It was a lot more than a sniff test.

Fence viewers also continued a community role that dated back several centuries.

It was an important matter to maintain fences and restrict livestock to their owners' properties. By the late 1800s, the job of fence viewer had changed a lot from colonial times, but Auburn still had three of them in 1883. A recent local news story told of a runaway donkey. If we still had fence viewers, that donkey might have stayed where it belonged.

Then there's the culler of staves. J.W. Chaplin held the title in 1883. Many decades earlier, residents of New England towns cut wood for barrel making, and the pieces (staves) were stacked in a communal pile. A "culler of staves" was appointed to inspect the pieces and throw out unusable wood.

There were also early examples of the Twin Cities' cooperation along the lines of current exploration of joint services. The old annual report talked about cooperation between the fire departments of Lewiston and Auburn. Lewiston's crews came to Auburn 125 years ago to help test the water pressure capabilities of the city's equipment.

My grandfather, Frederic Sargent, drove the school team, photographed here as students head off for a school day.

And school consolidation has been a hot-button topic all through the past century. The Auburn School Committee of 1883 said, "There are, in the opinion of your committee, too many and too small rural ungraded schools."

And finally, I wondered, is there a modern counterpart to the tythingman? Auburn had two tythingmen in 1883, Freedom Haskell and Daniel Lara. Their duties descended from days when towns set up groups of ten family units (a tythe) to watch out for common safety and law enforcement. Tythingmen were responsible for the general morals of the community, as well as observance of the Sabbath. They supervised liquor sales and reported on idle or disorderly persons, profane swearers or cursers and Sabbath breakers. Tythingmen also were empowered to stop unnecessary travel on the Sabbath. That's an office that has since disappeared, or at least its concerns have shifted away from governmental oversight.

THE VERY FIRST SETTLERS

For Native Americans, waterways were the highways, and networks of trails were the connectors in their complex transportation system. Lake Auburn's water flowed down a brook to the Androscoggin. Taylor Pond's outlet flowed to the Little Androscoggin and then to the big river. The Dead River, the Nezinscot, the Sabattus and many more streams are tributaries to the Great Androscoggin, and for centuries, these streams provided transportation and food for people of a forgotten culture.

My family's riverside woodlot land held some interest for governmental agencies seeking evidence of prehistoric settlements. Some initial digs unearthed a few interesting finds but nothing of great significance. The archaeologists discovered fire-split stones that indicated a hearth. They found a lot of things that seemed inconsequential, like a few burned seeds, a broken scraper and some ceramic bits and pieces.

The reports they gave us said that radiocarbon dating placed the activity in two prehistoric periods. The first was as many as two thousand years ago in what was called the early Middle Woodland period. The second was four to nine hundred years later in the—get this brain twister—"late Middle Woodland to early Late Woodland period."

That time may seem lost in the hazy past, when members of tribes we call Abenaki and Anasaguntacook were the only people of this area. Sometimes we're reminded of it through names with Native American origins, and our connections to the people who were here first are much closer than we may have thought.

Nancy Lecompte of Lewiston, also known as Canyon Wolf, is founder and director of Ne-Do-Ba, a nonprofit organization dedicated to exploring and sharing the Wabenaki history of Western Maine. Lecompte's book, *Alnôbak*, has a wealth of detail about this area and many real people of Native American ancestry.

From Lecompte's book, I learned about *Amitgonpontook*, an aboriginal "City on the Androscoggin." It was the Indian settlement on Auburn's Laurel Hill near the confluence of the Little Androscoggin and the bigger river. There's a lot of detail about artifacts found there and of a 1690 march and attack on the Native American settlement by Major Benjamin Church.

I also learned about Sockalexis (Jacques Alexis) Gabriel, possibly of Penobscot descent, who lived in this area just fifty to seventy-five years ago. He was known for his basket making and for his skills in the woods. The log cabin he built and lived in on the Holbrook Road in the Turner and North Auburn area still existed in recent years. Though his death occurred elsewhere, he is buried at North Auburn Cemetery.

Lecompte also shares in her book the following tale:

> *One day an Indian came to the house and asked to borrow a gun. The Indian explained there was a moose in the pasture which he would like to shoot. Mr. Jackson was a little reluctant to give a weapon to an Indian, but did so anyway. The Indian shot the moose, returned the gun, and left some moose meat for the family as a thank you.*

This little story from Lecompte's book is an account of an incident that took place on the Ferry Road in Lewiston sometime in the 1780s. A man whose ancestors settled in the Ferry Road area contributed it as

An old postcard shows rock profiles of two faces on the Great Falls that have since disappeared.

oral history. The story evokes a traditional image of Native Americans sharing their bounty with settlers. We tell a story with a similar theme at Thanksgiving every year, knowing that it is mostly fiction and is uncomfortable for Native Americans.

Those are considerations that are very important to Lecompte and the goals of her organization, Ne-Do-Ba. Her writing emphasizes the difficulty in separating fact from fiction. She warns us about early historians, some of whom might have had a political agenda that clouded their objectivity. In one sense, that story of early Lewiston is just interesting local lore. On another level, repeating that anecdote risks contributing to simplistic or just plain wrong ideas about Native Americans.

LEGENDS OF WEST PITCH

Almost as soon as European settlers put down roots in this part of the state, there were stories about Indian raids and war parties coming down the Androscoggin. There are at least three stories about deceit and death at West Pitch on the Auburn side of the falls in early colonial years.

We don't hear much about those tales these days, but eighty to one hundred years ago, everyone told stories of how white settlers were saved from the marauding Indians. In some versions, local heroes moved torches or bonfires marking the dangerous falls, and the warriors' canoes were swept over the falls in the darkness. A Joseph Weir, from Turner or Scarborough, is sometimes named as the one who moved the markers in revenge for a massacre of his family.

Stories like this are a very small slice of history. They may be true, or they may be colored by many cultural barriers and misunderstandings. These legends are told time and again with harmless intent but have been a source of discomfort to Nancy Lecompte. She presented a talk at a meeting of the Androscoggin Historical Society in which she debunked the florid accounts of mass mayhem at the falls. Lecompte noted the white-man-hero-versus-Indian-villain themes, and she cast doubt on any need to have fires marking a spot that would be well known to the area's natives. However, Lecompte said she could see the possibility of canoes engaging in a game of "chicken" above the falls, and a tragic mishap to one or more could have occurred.

My father's lifelong passion for poetry gave rise to yet another twist on this piece of history. In a poem called "Myth of West Pitch," he wrote about "a restless Indian princess who betrayed her tribe for the love of a white trapper."

He imagined how she moved the signal fires and caused her tribe's warriors to be swept over the falls. Tragically, her "faithless trapper" abandoned her, and "a leap to the roaring cascade was her only way to atone."

So what's wrong with a little embroidery in the telling of a good story? Twisted history can haunt us for generations. Today's descendants of Franco-American heritage are doing excellent work to correct many inaccuracies about their role in L-A's past. All of us can learn more and help to convey the honest truth.

We also have new neighbors here, and we don't fully understand them. We owe it to ourselves and to the Somali community to learn more about their culture and Islam, and the Somali families need to think about how they can make their lives open, interesting and collaborative with others.

It's fun to unravel legends and find the half-truths woven into them. But it's important to remember that a half-truth is a half-lie, and some not-so-subtle agenda could be the unfortunate basis of some enhanced stories.

GLIMPSES INTO OLD DIARIES

Sometimes a diary writer leaves us vivid images of a past age. Phebe Merrill of Hebron and Lewiston was such a person. Her diary of 1868, when she was thirty-two years old, contains a marvelous account of her feelings and attitudes.

Part of the year, she resided in Hebron, but much of her time was spent in Lewiston, where she worked in the Lincoln Block, a boardinghouse run by the Lewiston Mills Company for millworkers.

The diary is now in the keeping of the Androscoggin Historical Society. Here's some of what she wrote: "Jan. 12: Very cold. Suffered in church. Atwood B [Bumpus] read one of Spurgeon's sermons. I guess it was a good sermon, but a poor reader can spoil anything."

In February and March, Phebe talked about sewing carpet rags, more washing, an overnight visit from a linen peddler and maple sugar making. She noted on March 25 that "President Johnson's impeachment trial is progressing—rascal."

In August, Phebe left home to work in Lewiston:

Thurs., Aug. 6: A pleasant day. I arose at three, got ready, and Levi [her brother] *and I started for Lewiston about five. Got here about eight. It was hard to leave home. I have concluded to work in the kitchen of the boarding house.*

About two weeks later, Phebe wrote:

A very busy day—extra dishes and kitchen floor to wash, but no extra pay. Tom Thumb [the tiny showman who gained world-wide fame in tours arranged by P.T. Barnum] *is in the city. I got a glimpse of his coach and ponies from my window.*

In September, Phebe said:

A new cook, Mrs. Hellar from Rockland, came last night. She is not a religious woman, I find by her talk. She goes to dancing school. I was shocked, for she must be fifty years old, I should think, and she is a DEMOCRAT.

Phebe's work was hard, as her entry for September 29 shows:

This day I have made 37 pumpkin pies. Mrs. Lowell came down and rolled mince pie crust awhile—a great help—so we made 78 pies today, and that is not half the work we have done. Quite a scene in the kitchen in consequence of putting up "a mean dinner" for a man. I got some "sauce" from his wife. I consider her too low to be noticed.

Around Thanksgiving, she wrote, "I bid adieu to Lincoln Block and its inhabitants for awhile, and here I am with my mother."

What might you have to tell us in your diary today?

STAGECOACH—BUT NOT THE WESTERN KIND

What if legendary film director John Ford had made a movie about Maine? What if Ford's classic *Stagecoach* had featured a tavern in Danville instead of a Wild West outpost?

In fact, this famous native of Cape Elizabeth said on a 1947 visit to Portland that he often thought he would like to find a Maine story for his distinctive silver screen treatment. Some inspiration for his *Stagecoach* with

John Wayne could have come from Ford's youth, when the stages still ran from Portland to the Sebago area.

Stagecoach routes in early Maine had a lot of the adventure and romance immortalized by Pony Express exploits and harrowing adventures aboard stagecoaches in the West. They were symbols of the days when mail delivery was taking on new importance in the daily lives of American citizens and in the exploding world of business and industry.

According to *History of Androscoggin County* published in 1891, a man named Samuel Nash probably provided the first mail service to Lewiston. Around 1830, he traveled between Augusta and Portland three times a week on a route that took him through Greene. He drove a gig, a light two-wheeled, one-horse carriage.

John Ford might have found just the right character for a classic motion picture right here in Androscoggin County, but it's not Nash I'm thinking of. It would be Thomas Longley, a young man who came to Greene in 1810 and, some twenty years later, took over Nash's mail route.

The old history book calls Longley "the beau ideal of a dashing driver, courteous and obliging, tall and commanding in experience," and it continues, "he had a wonderful memory, and it is said that in the many errands entrusted to him he never made a memorandum and never forgot the smallest detail."

Furthermore, the book reveals, "He was a marvelous story-teller and the aroma of his narrations yet lingers in the atmosphere of places along his route."

Doesn't that make you wonder what Ford might have done with John Wayne or Henry Fonda in such a role?

Longley's stage started from Augusta in the morning. It reached Lewiston by noon and was in Portland by nightfall. Changes of horses were made at Winthrop, Greene and Gray.

The old history book notes, "The stage met the Farmington stage at Littlefield's Tavern in Danville because two coaches were often needed to accommodate passengers going to Portland."

After his days on the mail and coach runs, Longley "left the box" and became a hotel keeper in Portland. He sold the route to Squire Edward Little, who in turn sold it to Charles Clark.

Some of the other "whips" who ran the early stagecoach runs were Longley's son, Benjamin, and Lewis Howe of Leeds, as well as Albion C. Howard and Benjamin Beede.

By the mid-1800s, the prestige of the stagecoach lines had been diminished by the growth of railroads. Probably the last of the stage drivers was Phineas Clough, "for many years seated on the box of the Turner and Livermore stage."

Horseback mail delivery preceded the stagecoaches. As early as 1793, a new road from Augusta through Greene to Portland was speeding mail delivery by the adventurous postriders.

The mail was carried in a pouch behind the saddle, and riders had another bag with local mail. They received extra pay for that.

Riders galloped up to stations along the way, blowing a long tinhorn as they approached so there would be no time wasted as they changed horses.

Josiah Smith was this area's first postrider, followed by John Walker, who served towns from Livermore to Danville every week.

Although westerns were the movies that earned John Ford his fame, he might have found enough inspiration for yet another great film depicting an adventurous chapter in early days along the Androscoggin.

MOTORING WITH THE EARLY GPS

They used to call it motoring. The acquisition of an automobile was a particularly prestigious event for well-to-do members of the community in the early 1900s. Early spring was challenging for those proud automobile owners. For the most part, they had not been able to drive their vehicles on snow-covered Maine roads, and now the urge was building to get out and go touring on springlike days over barely passable unpaved roads.

Just before World War I, many of the automobiles seen around town were open to the elements. The adventurous automobilists often donned long coats and goggles for protection against dust or mud. They grabbed their GPS's and set off down the road like Mr. Toad in *The Wind in the Willows*.

Automobile travel was an adventure in the early days when road conditions were uncertain. Travel guides warned when certain routes should be avoided in wet weather.

Wait a minute. They grabbed a GPS?

Well, sort of. I have one. Maybe it was not a Global Positioning System, but it was a Geographical Positioning System. I found it in one of my frequent trash-or-treasure searches through boxes of old photos and letters.

The Maine Automobile Association, which was based in Portland, published yearly guides of motoring routes around the Pine Tree State, and the 1916 edition I came across is a remarkable forerunner of the digital screen with voice-assisted maps that we use today.

The title page says that the four-hundred-page book "points the way" to Maine's cities and towns, with almost mile-by-mile instructions on getting there. As you read, you can almost hear that electronic voice of a modern GPS. The book claims a tourist could cover the full "Pine Tree Tour" in less than two weeks.

Here's a sample of what's found in the pages of this four-inch-wide and ten-inch-tall volume.

At the start of directions to Farmington, the guide takes the driver past Lake Auburn and through Livermore Falls with notes about the route at frequent intervals. At the entry for mile 36.1 at North Jay, it says, "Cross bridge and pass monument on left." At East Wilton, mile 39.1, it says, "Keep left at fork at stone watering trough."

That's the kind of information listed for travel throughout Maine. The section describing Auburn-to-Portland says you will find "splendid new gravel road" from Auburn to Danville Junction and then "fair to good dirt road" to Portland. Some routes warn about poor travel in wet weather.

There's a box with the following advice midway through the book:

> *Remember that the preservation of the highways depends as much on the automobilist as it does on the road patrolman. Don't speed. Don't run in a rut. Keep off the shoulders as much as possible. Don't go around corners fast. Use chains only when necessary and don't apply your brakes too suddenly.*

The *Lewiston Journal* of May 16, 1916, carries an advertisement for Cadillac Sales Co., Park Street, Lewiston, that says a Twin Cities motorist "went out on those bad roads north of the town last Sunday, and made every hill on high."

There's also an ad for Hudson cars, which could be bought at the Hudson Motor Sales Co. on Main Street, Lewiston, and the Maxwell could be purchased at Hall & Knight Hardware Co. on Lisbon Street. Does the name Maxwell ring a bell? Jack Benny's old Maxwell could be heard coughing to a start on many of the comedian's radio shows.

A news item from May 1916 creates a vivid picture of motoring in 1916. It says that two men from Oxford were passing through Shaker Village at night. They had turned to the side to "let a team" pass, as many horse-drawn vehicles were still using the roads at that time.

The car "skidded into the ditch and almost in the twinkling of an eye the machine turned turtle, pinning the two men beneath."

Their shouts roused residents of the Shaker community, and one of the sisters said, "Not only did they cry for 'help,' but they also shouted, 'Murder!'"

The Shaker sisters and brethren righted the car, treated the men's cuts and bruises and gave them breakfast in the morning.

Motoring was truly an adventure nearly one hundred years ago as you followed the guidance of your paper-bound version of a GPS.

LAKE GROVE—A MAGICAL PLACE

There are so many things I wish I could have seen years ago. Lake Grove at East Auburn is one of them. It was a magical place.

I have seen old postcards that picture Lewiston-Auburn residents in late Victorian dress enjoying picnics or evening plays at this popular park beside Lake Auburn. I have read that it featured a menagerie with monkeys, an Arctic owl and a variety of wild animals native to this area. The grounds also boasted a bowling area, a well-groomed lawn for croquet and a horseshoe court.

Just as Memorial Day now fills our highways with families ready to put the cold winter and wet spring days behind them, warmer weather drew

The Lake Grove waterfront, shown in an old postcard, attracted thousands of visitors who rode horse-drawn and electric trolleys to its attractions.

throngs of area residents to that late 1880s amusement park on the shore of Lake Auburn. The rich and famous of the Victorian era would arrive at Lewiston's Grand Truck Railway terminal to take stagecoaches to the luxurious Poland Spring Hotel, but local folks flocked to Lake Grove in Auburn and Island Park in Lewiston.

Lake Grove offered only picnic grounds and a small zoo at first, but restaurants soon appeared. Before long, an outdoor theatre attracted large audiences, a dance hall echoed to bands from as far away as New York and a one-hundred-foot L-shaped dock offered rental canoes and boats to patrons, as well as steamer rides across the lake.

Research and writings of my aunt, Edith Labbie, brought vivid detail to the descriptions of Lake Grove that she collected in the 1970s. She said, "Asking people what they remembered about Lake Grove was like opening a box of happiness." The stories she heard revealed "what it meant to a community where shops and mills ate up so much time that there was a bright hilarity to the hours snatched for amusement."

Lake Grove House was a fine hotel that stood near the Lake Grove amusement area entrance.

The original dance pavilion had a wide piazza around it. On Sundays, the Lafayette Band gave morning and afternoon concerts.

The large Lake Grove House, a hotel where many performers stayed, stood near the Lake Grove grounds in East Auburn. Towering oak trees are long gone, and pines now stand where a busy state boat launch provides access to Lake Auburn.

What was it that contributed most to such a destination's success? Transportation—and in that day, it was the trolley. Both horse-drawn and electric trolleys were significant factors in Lake Grove's growth and also its decline. Building and promoting a fun-focused destination at the end of the line provided the incentive for patrons to drop their coins in the trolley fare boxes. Trolleys were a delightful mode of travel for city dwellers who could not afford to keep horses. Eventually, the automobile replaced them.

In 1881, two out-of-state investors brought $100,000 to L-A and founded the Lewiston-Auburn Horse Railroad Company. The horses were stabled on French Street (now Lake Auburn Avenue), where a corn factory was later built. There were ninety-two strong horses still there when electric trolleys were introduced in 1895.

The first horsecar route connected the head of Lisbon Street to the Maine State Fairgrounds on Lewiston's outer Main Street. It also went to the Perryville area (Turner, Summer and Center Streets today) in Auburn.

The early horsecars were called bobtails because they were quite stubby and could only seat about six. The driver pulled a cord to open the back door, and "the patron dropped his money in the cash box if he was honest; if not, a metal button did the trick." The fare was a nickel within city limits and three cents for a child. The fare covered admission to the grounds, while other visitors had to pay for their entrance.

Descriptions said, "The days of Puritanism were past and laughing girls in gowns top-heavy with leg-of-mutton sleeves and young men in straw skimmers flew across lots on swaying trolley cars."

Lake Grove's beginnings coincided with the 1883 extension of the Lewiston Horse Railroad Company's lines to East Auburn. There, the company established a lakeside pleasure spot. It was an early "If you build it, they will come" concept that led to these mini-theme parks, and it was a common practice in many communities.

What amazes me is the apparent ease with which families flocked to the popular local destination that was not far from my family's farm. Many families came "by team"—their own horse-drawn wagons of many styles. Downtown dwellers caught the horsecar or, later, the "electrics." These trolleys served L-A and its surrounding areas through summer and winter from the pre–Civil War period until automobiles essentially crowded them off the roads.

"Trips to 'The Grove' in open-air cars were festive occasions. Singing passengers packed the cars. More adventurous patrons even rode on the roofs." That was how my aunt, Edith Labbie, described trips to Lake Grove. In her columns in the *Lewiston Evening Journal* magazine section, she wrote often about Lake Grove. Her extensive accounts of Lake Grove were condensed into a section she contributed to the book *Auburn 1869–1969: 100 Years a City*, published by the Auburn History Committee in 1968.

Her vivid accounts came from family recollections, so I also heard bits and pieces of my grandparents' tales about the long-ago lakeside attraction.

"One weekend, 1,400 passengers made the round-trip," Labbie wrote. "Car patrons were admitted to Lake Grove without charge. Other visitors bought tickets after they hitched their horses to trees and fence posts."

You could buy a quart of peanuts for a nickel at J.W. Merrill's restaurant on the grounds. You could rent a boat or a canoe, and the boathouse walls were covered with tracings of record-sized salmon taken from Lake Auburn.

The cross-lake fare was fifteen cents on the steamer *Lewiston*, captained by Frank R. Whitney, but excursion rates were only a nickel. For the more affluent boat passengers, a stop for dinner at the Lake Auburn Mineral Spring Hotel on the west shore of the lake was in order. They returned to Lake Grove for the evening band concerts. The day might conclude with a ride on a buckboard driven by S.H. Briggs to the top of nearby Mount Gile, where patrons climbed to the top of a five-story observation platform to watch the sunset.

People and Recreation

Just a year after the opening of Lake Grove, E.T. Gile bought twelve acres of land on White Oak Hill Road in East Auburn across from today's municipal beach and park. He renamed the site after himself and cleared an area for the observatory. It offered a spectacular view of the White Mountains, the Poland Spring Hotel, the state fair trotting park and the Androscoggin River for twenty-five miles upstream.

"Lake Grove continued to prosper long after the Mount Gile facilities were closed," my aunt's articles said.

> *As the years went by, the Grove became a popular place for Chatauqua programs, lodge picnics, revivals, and political rallies. Skating parties were sponsored in the winter. The ice was scraped and illuminated. Accordion music and hot cocoa added to the pleasures.*
>
> *The outdoor theater at Lake Grove accommodated 500 patrons. It had a covered stage flanked by dressing rooms. Patrons sat on backless benches. In the event of showers, the lucky ones raised their umbrellas. Others held newspapers over their heads.*

Tickets for the shows were a dime in the afternoon and twenty cents in the evening, with new shows weekly. The presentations might be the Alabama Troubadours, an impersonation of Harry Lauder or the Powder Puff Review.

One intriguing production that my aunt mentioned was a reenactment of the Havana Harbor sinking of the battleship *Maine* staged by the trolley company. Was this an extravaganza of explosions and a scuttled barge in the waters of the lake, or was it all done onstage?

The last horsecar left the stable on French Street (now Lake Auburn Avenue) in 1895, and "the electric trolley was the new marvel." It marked the beginning of a changing era, in which roadsters appeared, flappers danced the Charleston and the Black Bottom and Lake Grove became a dance hall. On Sundays, when dancing was prohibited, there were free showings of silent movies.

The earliest Lake Grove development was such a success that the trolley company built Island Garden on an island on the Lewiston side of the falls. A lease was signed with Union Water Power Company in 1890, and a steel suspension bridge was constructed with new electrical lighting as a special attraction.

A two-hundred-seat theatre was built on the island. There was another building for hawkers who sold novelty items and food and a building where small wild animals were shown.

Programs at Island Garden changed weekly. There were plays, as well as many oddities that included a visit by a remarkable horse with a mane fourteen feet long, a forelock ten feet long and a tail of twelve feet.

One year, when rains had swollen the flow of the Androscoggin, a play was scheduled, but the bridge was swaying wildly above the water. The actors decided to go ahead with the play, and patrons were loyal enough to cross the bridge without incident.

It was the speed, economy and ease of new electric trolleys to Lake Grove at East Auburn that spelled the end for Island Garden.

There were four other significant recreation centers between Lewiston-Auburn and Brunswick in the days of horse-drawn trolleys and electric trolley companies.

Merrymeeting Park in Brunswick was the largest of the area's entertainment parks. Lisbon had its popular Frost Park, but it was Lake Grove that lasted the longest.

Frost Park, at the homestead of George D. Frost, sat atop a hill in Lisbon Falls. It had a dining room for forty and a large dancing pavilion. Each had huge stone fireplaces. A full-course dinner was fifty cents, and lobsters were twenty-five cents each in the earliest days.

There also was an amphitheatre for plays, benches with river and mountain views and swings with three seats suspended from one-hundred-foot trees.

It was a great place for political speeches and annual picnics of local companies and organizations. One 1924 outing by United Commercial Travelers of L-A included a Cundy's Harbor clambake and a return to Frost Park for games, songs and dancing. There were stocking-foot races, a fat man's contest, nail-driving contest, tug-of-war and a three-legged race. Also described was a tub race across the dance floor; three people with brooms for oars propelled the tubs across the pavilion. There was a baked bean supper, and the day ended with an oyster stew.

All this came to an end when Frost Park's pavilion caved in during the winter of 1926.

By 1928, Lake Grove had been losing money for some time. Automobiles gave families many more options for entertainment and travel. Lake Grove's end came in 1928, and the 160 cottages around the complex were sold off at ridiculously low prices. One of the fanciest cottages went under the auction hammer for twenty-five dollars.

The electric trolleys stopped running in 1941, but the Lewiston-Auburn Transit Company ran its buses with a "Lake Grove" destination sign for many years.

SPRINGWATER DREAMS

To some, it would be considered a blessing. Others would call it an unfortunate set of circumstances that put a cork in Auburn's chances of becoming a big player in today's worldwide multibillion-dollar bottled water boom.

The stories of Poland Spring's glory days are well known. It was a period in the mid- to late 1880s when celebrities flocked to the fashionable resort at the site of the famous springhouse.

One of the area's lesser-known might-have-beens is the Auburn Mineral Spring Company and an ill-fated hotel at West Auburn that aimed for similar fame and fortune.

Dana B. Holmes, a respected early resident of East Auburn, was a principal force in the project on Lake Auburn's west shore, not far from where he was born in North Auburn around 1840. Holmes left his father's farm at the age of fourteen, and for more than twenty years he was a part of Auburn's earliest shoemaking days. It was a time when there were no factories. Just about every farm had a small shop where family members assembled shoe parts that they took in from the shoe companies.

They could make between seven and fifteen dollars a week, according to L.C. Bateman, who was Grange editor of the *Lewiston Evening Journal*. In the early 1920s, Bateman wrote about Holmes, early shoemaking and the West Auburn Hotel and spring.

In the early 1880s, Holmes was first employed by the Auburn Mineral Spring Company. The company was formed to tap into a spring that had been found to have pure water and an inexhaustible flow. Its history dated to 1876, when typhoid fever blamed on impure water hit many families in West Auburn. The spring was acclaimed for its curative powers.

Holmes said he measured the spring's flow at 28 gallons a minute (nearly 5 million gallons a year). That's a respectable rate compared to Poland Spring's extraction of almost 500 million gallons in 2005 from its six sites in Maine.

Agents for the Auburn Mineral Spring Company sold stock all over New England, New York and Philadelphia. A small hotel was built at the site, and the company paid $5,000 to a Bath firm to build a large side-wheel, steam-powered boat known as the *Lady of the Lake*. It was used to ferry passengers across Lake Auburn from the old horse railroad at Lake Grove in East Auburn to the West Auburn Hotel.

The operation flourished for a while, but business slipped to the point where lawyers were called in to settle affairs. Holmes bought up tax deeds on the property and reorganized the business.

In an interview with Bateman, Holmes said, "It was decided to build a new hotel and use the old one for an ell and a cook room, with bedrooms for the help. This new hotel was a fine structure and was hardly finished in 1893 when it took fire and was burned to the ground."

He speculated that rubbish in the basement was ignited "by spontaneous combustion or a spark of fire fell from the keeper's pipe. At any rate, it went up in smoke and that ended the dream of a great resort."

After the hotel burned, Holmes and a hired man continued work at the springhouse making ginger ale.

"The bottling house was a good-sized structure and we could put up 14 barrels of water at a time," Holmes said. "With more capital and fewer owners to dictate, it might be running today and doing a big business."

So it goes. There's no grand hotel on the shores of Lake Auburn today, but there's still evidence of it. Not long ago, my wife, Judy, and I hiked with a couple of friends along a closed road on the lake's west shore. We then walked into the woods a short distance. There, almost invisible until you were right in front of it, was a massive wall about twelve feet high and fifty or more feet long. It was made of huge stone blocks, and when compared to old photos of the hotel, it was obvious that this was the foundation of that ill-fated venture.

THE GREAT DEPARTMENT STORE

If Bradford Peck, the founder of "the Great Department Store" in Lewiston, were alive today, he might be saying, "I told you so." After all, Peck had a theory that the whole world could be run on the same principles that you would use to manage a big department store.

At Christmastime, longtime residents recall many welcome signs of Christmas in L-A, and the five-story B. Peck Department Store on Main Street at the head of Lisbon Street was at the center of it all. The historic store—the largest in New England outside Boston when it was built in 1899—was thriving around the middle of the 1900s.

Marvelous life-sized animated Christmas displays appeared in the large storefront windows. Decorations filled the store's five floors, and even the overhead maze of piping for the pneumatic tube cash transport system was festooned in garland and glitter. Shoppers thronged Hulett Square and surged in and out of the twin revolving doors at Peck's main entrance.

For most of us young customers, the primary destination at Peck's was the basement level. That's where Santa held court on his throne overlooking the fishpond—a round enclosure filled with wrapped presents where (for a fee) a kid could snag some likely treasure with the little fishing pole supplied by the supervising elves.

Of course, this yearly ritual didn't come without its downside. The lines were long, it was very noisy and it was incredibly hot under all that winter clothing.

Nevertheless, mothers from miles around endured this for the sake of their youngsters' minute or two on Santa's lap—and that flash of the store's official camera to immortalize the moment.

That remarkable store at "the head of the street" paralleled Peck's high ambitions, if not his precise utopian vision. Wallace Evan Davies wrote about Peck's life in the December 1947 edition of the *New England Quarterly*. He said Peck's life was a "Horatio Alger pattern" of rags-to-riches accomplishment.

Peck was born in the Charlestown district of Boston in 1853. He left school at the age of twelve to become an errand boy at the large Jordan Marsh's department store. He later was vice-president of the Joliet Dry Goods Co. in Illinois.

Peck's book, *The World a Department Store*, was self-published in 1900 as an initial step in launching a social experiment known as the Cooperative Association of America.

Peck set his utopian novel in Lewiston. There, in 1900, his protagonist, a harassed capitalist whom Peck named Percy Brantford, took a double dose of a sleeping powder that put him in a coma for twenty-five years, according to an outline of the book from Cornell University.

"On his awakening in 1925, he found his native city transformed under a system of cooperative enterprise that had replaced the capitalistic system with which he was familiar," the outline said.

In his book, Peck described his utopian view of Lewiston. He wrote, "Mr. Brantford, looking out of his parlor windows, was aesthetically impressed with the view before him." He recalled big city tenements, and said, "Here these old-time back yards, so familiar to him, were transformed into a regular system of parkways...and it seemed as if Paradise dawned before him."

The book has ten line drawings of the new Lewiston that Peck envisioned. He includes a detailed plan of a typical city block with sites for eight apartment buildings. Streets were laid out in grids with occasional diagonal streets and numerous parks. He also had a plan for neighborhood financial cooperatives to make all this happen.

Although Peck's utopian dream may still be considered under development, his store prospered for a good part of his life. Recession took a toll on profitability, and Peck's closed in 1982. Since 1988, the building has been home to an L.L. Bean telephone order center.

CHRISTMAS CROWDS AT THE HEAD OF THE STREET

There's nothing I like better than going through the pages of old newspapers and spotting some news item or ad that triggers a long-forgotten image in my mind. Some of the clearest recollections come from the years of my early boyhood, when Christmas in L-A was a real wonderland.

Was my memory accurate? Were there really throngs of shoppers on Lisbon Street sidewalks? Were there traffic jams at downtown intersections?

Yes, indeed. Three days before Christmas 1951, the Lewiston Police Department was reporting the busiest traffic of the season, and every available officer was assigned to traffic duty. Several streets had to be made one-way.

In my favorite kind of free-form research, I picked a couple of years (1953 and 1954) and scanned those December newspapers. I was looking for the forgotten details of that time I knew as a boy, but I was also looking for similarities.

The details included throngs of pre-Christmas shoppers at "the head of the street," where Lisbon Street meets Main Street. If you were coming from Auburn, you talked about "going overstreet."

Traffic stopped for red lights, and dozens of people, especially on a Saturday, surged across the intersection. On one side, they explored the gift ideas at Peck's, and on the other side, they were visiting the five-and-dime stores: Woolworth's, J.J. Newberry and Kresge's. There are still echoes of those stores in faded signs and names spelled out by tiles at former sidewalk entrances.

Endless gift-giving options could be found on five floors at the large B. Peck Department Store—an imported French calf handbag for $10.00, wool gloves for $1.00 or Old Spice scents in toiletries for a dollar or two. Walking dolls were $1.98 and $2.98.

Those 1953 editions of the *Lewiston Daily Sun* also advertised the L.L. Bean canoe shoe, from its Freeport store, for $5.45. That's just one case where past and present intersect. After Peck's closed in 1988, the building became a call center for L.L. Bean catalogue shoppers, so the gift giving from that location continues today.

Next to Peck's were two stores that are still around and are now much bigger than they were then. There was a small J.C. Penney store and a Sears at the time when it was still known as Sears Roebuck and Company.

Liggett's Rexall Drugstore at the corner of Lisbon and Main was always busy. That's where city buses boarded full loads of passengers. A familiar sight there was the costumed Planter's Peanut man in front of a magnificently aromatic shop.

Dozens of quality women's clothing stores were located on Lisbon Street: Ward's, Reid & Hughes, Star, Senter's, Janelle's. Men's clothing stores there included Leblanc's and A.H. Benoit & Co. Louie's, a company that is still around, also did business then. In Auburn, Flander's and Cobb-Watson were respected men's clothing stores.

The second-floor ballroom of Lewiston City Hall reverberated every weekend of the late 1950s and early 1960s to the PAL Hop dances of the Police Athletic League. *Marcel Bonenfant photo.*

People and Recreation

Atherton Furniture is no longer in business, but a short distance from there, on Lincoln Street, F.X. Marcotte Furniture (originally labeled "undertaker and dealer in furniture and stoves") is well over one hundred years old now.

Christmas parties for companies and clubs were being held throughout the Twin Cities. People celebrated the season at the Mirimar Tearoom, Hotel Steckino, the Nanking, the Elm Hotel and the DeWitt Hotel.

On December 12, 1953, the nationally acclaimed Claude Thornhill Orchestra was at the Lewiston Armory for the Auburn Firemen's Ball. Tickets were $1.50. Local favorite Stevie Stephens was playing for a dance at Lewiston City Hall.

Hans Christian Anderson with Danny Kaye was opening at the Auburn Theatre, the Empire had Alan Ladd in *Drum Beat* and the double-bill at the Strand was *The Bounty Hunter* with Randolph Scott and *Outlaw's Daughter* with Bill Williams. *Three Coins in the Fountain* was at the Ritz.

Young people may roll their eyes when their elders start talking about the old days. They may wonder what in the world was so good about that era before iPods and instant messaging, but their memories will one day be just as important. Will it be a romantic dinner at Fuel, the upscale restaurant at the reclaimed Lyceum Hall on Lisbon Street where we once shopped at the Berry Paper Co. store? Will it be fun with friends at the Auburn Mall or the multi-screen movie theatres? The answers only come with time and the mystery of selective memory.

The old Lisbon Street is gone, but L-A's business and civic leaders are working hard to bring vitality to our cities. Once, the "head of the street" was the center of activity. That has changed and expanded, but there's no reason that future memories won't be just as wonderful.

Although our farm was not much more than a mile from downtown Auburn, it was still in the country, so those trips to town around Christmas were always a special event. When my brother and I were growing up on the Auburn farm, it was a tradition for our father to take us to our woodlot, about a mile upriver, where we would find and cut a seven-foot fir tree that we deemed suitable as the family's Christmas tree. There were some other traditions I was not aware of, and I learned of them when I read a column by my aunt, Edith Labbie, in a 1967 *Lewiston Evening Journal* magazine section.

Marshall's Popcorn Truck was a curbside fixture of the 1950s and '60s for high school dances at the Auburn YMCA or movies at the nearby Auburn Theatre.

She told how her mother, my grandmother, took sprigs of fir from the woodlot excursions of the early 1900s and placed them around the pictures throughout the house.

"The mounted buffalo horns that she brought back from North Dakota assumed a rakish air with the fir branch trimming," my aunt wrote.

Another tradition I had not heard about involved Christmas cards:

> *After breakfast, Mother brought out all the Christmas cards that had been arriving for several weeks. She never opened a single one until Christmas morning for she contended that it was a mechanical gesture if we mailed a card to this person or that because they had been missed in the original mailing. She felt it would be taken as an affront or an afterthought.*

We think of traditions as being set in stone, but they're really transitory things. Tomorrow's memories in Androscoggin County will most likely involve a drive to see the spectacular electric light displays or the muted beauty of a neighborhood bathed in light from hundreds of roadside luminaries.

So make the most of tradition, and remember that we're shaping future memories all the time.

The Old Grange Meeting

There are Grange Halls all over Maine. Some stand empty, awaiting sale or demolition; others have been converted to imaginative new uses; and some continue to attract enthusiastic members.

The Grange has provided important benefits to farm families through nearly 150 years, and it was an important part of my family's life.

The Grange has been an important organization for farm families through the years. My family supported Auburn Grange No. 4 at East Auburn.

Although I was never a member, the organization's social life and ritual mysteries made a deep impression on my preteen years in Auburn.

It was at Auburn Grange No. 4, near Lake Grove in East Auburn, where my grandfather honed his oratorical skills. Grange meetings were occasions for members to hold forth on all kinds of political and economic topics of the day, and Frederic S. Sargent was not shy about stating his opinions. He was a talker, and he liked nothing better than an audience of one or more to share his views.

Grange night was a special time in my early years. Youngsters got only brief glimpses of the formal meetings, and we wondered what we were missing. The doors would be closed, and the children of members would wait impatiently for the after-meeting fun and food.

Dances were popular events. After Saturday night meetings, there was always a Grand March in which all members paraded back and forth.

Amateur entertainments were popular at the Grange Halls. Here, male members dress up for a skit. My grandfather, father, brother and I are all in this group photo.

Then, a small orchestra—often only a woman at the upright piano and maybe a saxophone player—played old and new songs for the dancers.

That East Auburn organization had a rich heritage. A *Lewiston Evening Journal* news story of March 12, 1949, marked the seventy-fifth anniversary of what began as Auburn Grange. Its first location, for about a year, was the Grand Army Hall on Main Street.

Prior to Granges, there were Farmers' Clubs around the country where men and women met separately and debated agricultural and household issues, but they declined after the Civil War. The Grange, officially known as Patrons of Husbandry, was organized in Washington, D.C., in 1867. Its arrival in Maine occurred in 1873. The following year, the Maine State Grange was organized in Lewiston, and Auburn Grange was the fourth to be formed in the state. In three years, Maine had 228 Granges and about twelve thousand members.

Auburn Grange No. 4 is distinguished for its introduction of the nation's first "degree staff and auxiliary." Degree work, like traditions of most fraternal organizations, consisted of closed-door rituals that stressed lessons in morality, frugality and the value of honest work. My grandmother, Hattie Field Sargent, was among the members of that first auxiliary.

The newspaper account said that the hall's original entrance was by the back stairs, lit by kerosene lanterns placed in brackets. In later years, acetylene replaced kerosene, and eventually electricity was installed.

The front of the building housed a store. Group purchasing was one of the benefits of Grange membership. The store was discontinued in 1901, when the hall was enlarged and a front entrance was added.

In the early days, the women brought not only the food but also the dishes.

"The women wore calico dresses and the men cowhide boots and overalls to meetings, with the women sitting on one side and the men on the other," the news story said.

Fire destroyed the Grange Hall at East Auburn on March 9, 1927. It was rebuilt within a year.

Willard Waterman was a member of Auburn Grange No. 4 for sixty-one years, and the seventy-fifth anniversary history listed some of the things he did for the group. It said he changed water pipes from overhead to underground, constructed a septic tank in the cellar, did decorative inlay work on the wooden floor and even grew the wheat that was needed for ritual tableaus.

I have always been amazed to see many Grange Halls around the state that are nearly twins to Auburn Grange No. 4. They have a first-floor dining hall with a kitchen area at the back, and wide stairways lead to the second-floor meeting room. There's a stage for community shows, and sometimes wooden benches run along the side walls.

Now that the hall in East Auburn is gone (demolished a few decades ago for commercial construction on the site), I enjoy visiting the Norway Grange for shows by the Oxford Hills Music and Performing Arts Association. That hall still looks much like the one I remember.

The Poor Farm Was No Joke

"Two dollars for that? What are you trying to do? Put me in the poor farm?" It was a common complaint in the old days, much as it is today, although today the complaint is more likely to contain jokes about bankruptcy or a government bailout.

The poor farm was no joke. It was very real, and it was the end of the line for many unfortunate people whose circumstances put them at the mercy of the town.

There was a poor farm, or more often called a town farm, in Auburn dating back to about 1845. Any town that provided something for its poor or dependent residents was considered to be progressive and charitable, but the descriptions of what those provisions might be paint a very dismal picture.

In *Auburn 1869–1969: 100 Years a City*, Ralph B. Skinner, city historian, records many stark facts about the fate of paupers. There was no sugarcoated pretense that anyone prospered from welfare or government assistance in those days.

Skinner's 1968 book states that Auburn's first "town house" was at Young's Corner, the area near today's Lost Valley Ski Area. It was established in 1845, about three years after Auburn split off from Minot. Within a short time, residents were advocating a "town farm," because the residents could raise some food and contribute toward their own upkeep.

Before that happened, Auburn's system for caring for the indigent was similar to a practice common in early New England. It was called "bidding them off" to other townspeople for board and keep. Those who could do no work at all (young children or widows with children) received some special arrangements from the overseers of the poor.

In 1845, Auburn had nine dependent persons, and twelve others were bid off at auctions. Skinner's book said that an effort was made to keep couples and family groups together in neighborhoods they knew.

"An elderly woman and a man, unable to work, were bid off separately for 75 cents a week, or approximately $39 a year, which was a much higher rate than that of all of the others," Skinner wrote.

One middle-aged widow, able to do some housework, brought an offer of $26 a year, and in the case of one housework-able young woman, the bidder asked the town to pay him only 29 cents a week for her keep, or $15 a year.

Land and buildings for Auburn's first poor farm were attained in 1848. The land was a seventy-five-acre tract on the south slope of Maple Hill known as the Tribou Farm.

Other sites came later, including a seventeen-year duration at a farm across from Taber's lakeside stand and driving range on Lake Shore Drive. Remains of the farm's foundation were found when a residence was built there in 1967.

Descriptions of a fire apparently refer to that farm: "Between five and six o'clock on the afternoon of July 26, 1873, while the 17 inmates were at supper, there came a heavy electrical storm. The barn was struck by lightning and was soon engulfed in flames."

Newspaper accounts said that "the inmates were taken for temporary shelter to Bearce House, a rooming house built by Horace Bearce for his employees behind his shoe factory at Auburn Hollow." That was a neighborhood name given to North Auburn at the time, and a Grange Hall was built later on the Bearce House site.

The farm couldn't be rebuilt, and the city bought the Henry Stetson farm on Upper Turner Street. Its use as the city farm continued through 1964. The site eventually came to be the home of Central Maine Community College.

In the later years of the last city farm, Rex V. Bridges was the well-known superintendent. He also had been Androscoggin County sheriff.

Bridges had been brought up on big farms in the Midwest, and he took over the Auburn operation in 1924. Under Bridges and his wife, Geneva, the farm provided cash from garden sales. It also provided hay for twenty-four horses in the city's fire and highway departments, but it was garbage collection and hog raising that brought in the money to keep the farm going. In the forty years under Bridges' management, the Auburn City Farm population ranged from a high of forty-six to only two when it closed in the 1960s.

THE OLD RADIO STATIONS

"On the air" entered the nation's vocabulary in the early 1920s, as radio became the newest popular sensation.

It was 1922 when Maine's first licensed radio station appeared, and it was in Auburn. That pioneering effort was known as WMB, and it lasted only a short time. Nevertheless, it captured the enterprising spirit that would lead to a rich broadcasting history in the Twin Cities.

The station originated through the scientific interest and enthusiasm of Elmer Nickerson and Thurl Wilson. Nickerson owned Auburn Electrical Company, a store on Court Street, as well as a battery and tire store at 95 Turner Street. Wilson, recently graduated from Edward Little High School, went to work for Nickerson in 1916.

The WMB story is told in the pages of *The History of Broadcasting in Maine* by Ellie Thompson, published about twenty years ago by the Maine Association of Broadcasters. It says that Wilson worked after hours and at his own expense at the battery store to build his own transmitting set. Wilson sent out his personal brand of programming. He recited poetry such as "The Face on the Bar Room Floor," and he sang and played the mandolin and banjo.

Owners of crystal sets, who could pick up some faraway radio stations, complained that Wilson's signal was interfering with reception, and furthermore, they pointed out that neither the small station nor Wilson was licensed.

This was only a minor setback. Another Auburn resident, D. Wayne Bendix, did have a license to operate a broadcast station. In April 1922, the U.S. Department of Commerce issued Maine's first radio station license for WMB to Auburn Electrical Company with Bendix as operator and Wilson as assistant.

WMB became one of only twenty-four licensed radio station in the United States and the only one north of Massachusetts. That meant it was required to broadcast all government radio reports, including crop information, weather forecasts and all government speeches. The first official WMB program was an Arbor Day speech on Friday, April 18, 1922, which was repeated the next evening. The *Lewiston Evening Journal* announced:

> *Local doctors will deliver into the air special speeches on hygiene and care of the body, local bankers will speak on thrift and banking principles, (and there will be) orchestra selections, as well as addresses by prominent persons who have come to Auburn or Lewiston.*

The newspaper also mentioned ambitious plans that were extremely far-sighted. Reports said:

> *As now contemplated, the Auburn Electrical Company station will make wire connections with such place as the Lewiston City Hall when some famous speaker or well known singer is present, and will broadcast the speech or song, whichever the case may be.*

In May, the station moved into third-floor space at Auburn Hall, and a large L-shaped aerial was fitted over the street to accommodate broadcast of a speech dedicating the brand-new YMCA building on Turner Street. The next day, city officials ordered that it be taken down. The Androscoggin Electric Company of Lewiston had complained that the four-strand wire passed dangerously close over hundreds of power lines and trolley wires.

Another engineering problem involved the transmitter's twenty-four wire connections, which would overheat. This caused Wilson to shut down his broadcasting three or four times a night. Although the station's one-hundred-watt transmitter had a predicted fifty-mile range, the station received mail that said it was heard as far away as Denver, Colorado.

Commercials were not allowed, and when WMB plugged Lawrence Music Company, the station ran into license problems. Probably the main reason for WMB's end was the toll it took on Wilson. He had to work a full-time day job and then broadcast at night without pay.

Some reports say the station did not complete a full year of operation. Others say it ceased broadcasting sometime before 1926.

In later years, we tuned our tube-driven AM radios to WLAM and WCOU. It's really not so long ago that events around the Twin Cities came into our homes on airwaves and we found a comforting mix of local on-air personalities. Local radio stations started our days with breakfast chats and live music, followed by a full day of news, sports and entertainment. But it was mostly a case of "hear" today, gone tomorrow. Only occasional snippets of the everyday early broadcasts remain.

Walter Beaupre was one of those early broadcasters at WCOU. He shared stories of those days in articles he wrote in the early 1990s for *Radiogram*, a publication for enthusiasts of OTR (old time radio). His descriptions of behind-the-scenes antics at the station are delightfully candid and informative.

Beaupre was a freshman at Bates in 1944 when the college's famed debate and speech professor Brooks Quimby asked him, "Do you drink?" Somewhat befuddled, Beaupre replied that he did not drink, and Quimby said, "Then, would you be interested in a night announcer's job at WCOU?"

Beaupre explained that the job opening was the result of a recent fiasco in which he hinted at boredom and booze on the station's night shift. It seems, he said, "an announcer decided to put on the air a specially-made transcription announcing the end of World War II. The phony transcription featured the voices of President Roosevelt, and other dignitaries, thanking God for the sudden, unheralded Allied victory."

That lapse of judgment was called "a cruel hoax during the darkest hours of the war" in local news reports.

"WCOU apologized," Beaupre said.

He said most of the key personnel at the station were away in service to Uncle Sam. That included the owner, Faust Couture (from whose last name the call letters were taken), station manager and ace sportscaster John Libby, chief announcer Bob Payne and announcer/musician Laverne "Miff" Coulton.

"So it was business manager Oscar Normand who—all in one fateful evening—interviewed me for the job, showed me how to run the RCA console and turntables, pointed out the pile of commercial copy, watched me as I stumbled through the routine for a while, and left me to my own devices," Beaupre recalled.

When WCOU came on the air in 1938, it was one of only seven stations in Maine. It broadcast the Yankee and Mutual networks.

The Couture family (also owners of WFAU in Augusta) pioneered French-language newspapers in the United States. Beaupre recalled that the first floor of a Lisbon Street building housed the paper *Le Messager*, while business offices for the radio station took up most of the second floor, and the two studios and control room were on the third.

Live local shows were a staple of the broadcast day. Beaupre fondly remembered Roselle Coury, "a raven-haired song stylist from Berlin, N.H., who broke into radio by buying her own air time, selling spot announcements within her shows, and arranging for the additional musical talent. She drove the six hours from and to Berlin every day."

WCOU eventually hired her full time.

"Roselle Coury was a first class talent in every respect—a terrific speaking voice and a fine pop singer," Beaupre said. "There were few women, local or network, on the airwaves in the '40s and '50s any better than Roselle Coury."

Marion Payne Louisfell was Coury's frequent accompanist on the organ and Steinway grand in Studio 1, and she had a noontime show called *Gaslight Serenade*. She was a sister of Maine's U.S. senator Frederick G. Payne.

Beaupre said that WCOU was pioneering FM radio in 1947 when he had an idea for a stereo broadcast. Just place an AM and an FM radio a few feet apart in the same room and you had stereo sound of the dual-cast show he called *Conversations in Music*. One microphone picked up the Hammond organ and voice of Marion Payne Louisfell, and a second mic picked up Beaupre's voice and his piano playing.

He said it might have been the nation's first commercially sponsored thirteen-week series in stereo.

After his broadcast days, Beaupre became a University of Rhode Island educator. He was nationally known for his work on clinical methods for improving voice/speech instruction for the deaf, and in 1984, he wrote *Gaining Cued Speech Proficiency*, a manual that is still considered a leading text in the field.

Beaupre died in April 1998.

Details about another L-A radio station were found in a photo-filled booklet I bought for a dollar about thirty-five years ago: *WLAM: 25 Years of Broadcasting*, published in 1972 to commemorate that station's activities beginning in 1947.

The station's transmitter building stands empty now on Washington Street in Auburn, but the well-known "Studio A" of WLAM-AM at 129 Lisbon Street is long gone. From that site, many L-A residents will remember broadcasts of the *Alarm Clock Club* by WLAM's first morning man, Fred Haggerty. Later, Sonya Forgue and Denny Shute were featured on *Coffee Time*. At noon every Saturday there was a *Sidewalk Interviews* show.

WLAM was an affiliate of ABC Network, and a high point for the station was a week in August 1964, when the whole cast of *Don McNeill and the Breakfast Club* came to Lewiston High School auditorium for capacity-audience national broadcasts.

Other popular events were the *Foods with a Flair* cooking school shows from Lewiston City Hall and remotes from the annual Modern Living Show at the Lewiston Armory, as well as auto shows that featured new models from Kaiser, Henry J, Studebacker and DeSoto.

People and Recreation

Baby boomers are today's prime audience for golden oldies on the radio, but in the late 1940s, WLAM spun recordings of really old music—and it was spinning cylinders, not wax and vinyl platters. Lisbon's historian/humorist/author John Gould played selections from his antique collection on the *1470 Club* with Bob Demers and Les Hubley.

WLAM had a strong teen following in the 1950s. Every Saturday, Cecilia Butler and Fred Haggerty hosted the *Peck's Teen Age Coke Party* for live audiences of L-A's young people at Studio A. Frank Sweeney also was a popular afternoon DJ and sock hop host.

There was a Jeopardy-like quiz show for local teen contestants called *Prep Hall Question Corner* with Hal Dutch as emcee. It was a remote broadcast from Benoit's men's clothing store, and one week I was a contestant from Edward Little High School, along with Danny Sullivan of St. Dom's High School and Dan Calder of Lewiston High School. I think St. Dom's took the prize that week.

Another youth-oriented program was *Junior Town Meeting* moderated by Frank Wimmer, an Edward Little High School teacher.

In 1960, the station inaugurated live broadcasts of Lewiston City Council meetings—the first of its kind in Maine—but hometown sports have always been the strong suit for radio.

The old WLAM will be remembered for Bill Dey's *Sports Newsreel* and Cliff Gove's local sports notes and commentary. It was also the place to turn for many highlights of local sports history. WLAM was at Boston Garden when Lewiston High School's 1960 basketball team took a twenty-six-game undefeated streak to the New England tournament. The team lost the tournament game, which was reported live to L-A fans by Fred Gage and Parker Hoy.

For football fans, Hyme Shanahan, Paul Brogan and Parker Hoy were the voices of *Pepsi's Game of the Week*.

Dick Michelsen, Lewiston Raceway track announcer, will be remembered for his distinctive call of "They're at the head of the stretch!" as he reported the running of each harness racing season's second race and daily double results.

Legendary heavyweight boxing champion Joe Louis once visited the Lisbon Street studio for an interview.

I took this photo of President Lyndon B. Johnson when he addressed twelve thousand people at Lewiston's Kennedy Park on August 20, 1966.

It's interesting to find that call letters of radio stations have a kind of genealogy, thanks to licensing by the Federal Communications Commission. WLAM begat WKZN in 1990, which begat WZOU in 1993, which begat a Portland incarnation of WLAM in 2001. In Auburn, today's WEZR-1240 has a call letter history that can be traced back to Lewiston's WCOU, and it continues broadcasting's heritage of community involvement.

PART IV

War and Sport

THE GREAT WAR ENDS

"WAR IS AT AN END." Those words in two-inch-high bold black print shouted the news from the front page of the *Lewiston Daily Sun* on Monday morning, November 11, 1918. The Great War, which would become known as World War I, was over, and the Twin Cities were poised to erupt in jubilation.

A second headline under the report of armistice terms read, "Lewiston-Auburn Fittingly Celebrates Greatest Event in World History."

The story said that Lewiston's mayor declared a public holiday with "continuous celebration throughout the day." A monster bonfire was planned for the evening, when two hundred tar barrels were to be set ablaze. The location was described as "the public square," which would likely mean the area near Lewiston City Hall.

The news story said that an Associated Press telegraph transmission brought the news very soon after the armistice was signed at 2:45 a.m. The *Lewiston Daily Sun* staff immediately notified the mayors of the two cities, and they passed the wonderful news on to the fire and police departments. In minutes, fire whistles were sounding, soon joined by church bells and factory whistles.

The predawn excitement accelerated as hastily dressed residents drove through town with horns blaring and flags waving. Many people headed straight for the newspaper's offices on Park Street to be sure that the news was true and was actually posted on the public bulletin board. There had been many false rumors of peace in preceding weeks, and people tended to be skeptical.

As dawn broke, the cities' officials began preparations for a massive local celebration and parade. The mayors were said to have called the leaders of local bands and "ordered them and their organizations together as quickly as possible and to be ready for an all-day and all-night celebration." That line ended with a big WOW!

The parade began at 7:30 a.m., and just before that, the newspaper story said, "A.E. Smith of 171 Park Street, Lewiston, wearing the regalia of Uncle Sam, appeared at the Mayor's office and was assigned to a first position in the parade."

Two Lewiston aldermen were appointed to go to the home of Lew Morrill on Webster Street, where they were to "get a cannon and all the cartridges and fireworks Lew had on hand."

A cannon on the library lawn also was fired repeatedly for the occasion.

> *Thousands of people…men, women and children…marched in the parade. There were professional men walking side by side with the mill men clad in their working frocks and carrying dinner pails as they had come prepared to work before they knew that a PUBLIC HOLIDAY had been declared.*

Auburn's celebration was equally boisterous. It was reported that "Forest Potter was out at the first stroke of the bells with his big GMC truck." He made several runs to deliver fireworks and tar barrels that fueled big bonfires at "Court Square" and at the Engine House.

The report said the fires burned so furiously that "Bill Butterfield [presumably a police or fire department official] had to come over and warn the boys that they were stopping the cars."

The celebration continued well into the night.

Shot guns and revolvers were numerous and the young cannons at the Engine House added their vote to the uproar. Autos dragging tin pans and boilers were a feature of the noisy program, all being loaded with shouting girls and streaming flags.

Although L-A's citizens didn't know it at the time, that was the first celebration of what was originally known as Armistice Day and later became Veterans Day.

THE "Y GIRLS"

The front page of the *Lewiston Daily Sun* screamed "U.S. and Japan at War." It was December 7, 1941, and we had been plunged into a worldwide conflict once again. Those first hours were filled with fear and anxiety, and the surprise attack on Pearl Harbor in the Pacific brought understandable apprehension about the possibility of East Coast dangers. A Portland news item said that "hostile forces" were an hour outside Boston.

In the next few days, local officials sought to calm fears. Under the big bold headlines of war news, the *Lewiston Evening Journal* reported that increased defense measures were being taken for local industry, and recruiting offices were doing a "rush business." One *Lewiston Daily Sun* headline read, "Armed Guard at Gulf Island and Deer Rips Dams," and civilian defense organizations were calling urgent meetings. At that time, W. Scott Libbey, president of the Libbey Mill, was head of the local civil defense effort.

As wartime routines developed, many young women of the area came to Lewiston for employment. A group of them who called themselves the "Y Girls" got together for a reunion not long ago. The occasion marked a special friendship that began in the years of World War II when they were living at the YWCA building in Lewiston. That three-story brick building is now converted into apartments, but the memories of those days and nights more than sixty years ago are still fresh.

Throughout World War II, gasoline was rationed. Ration stamps such as these issued to my father determined how much fuel auto owners could purchase.

I was privileged to listen in, at their invitation, as seven ladies who were mostly in their eighties renewed acquaintances and caught up on news. They met at a local restaurant, as they have done about ten times since they first reconnected around 1973.

The war was far from the Twin Cities, but life for everyone underwent extraordinary adjustments in those years. Gasoline was scarce, and the young people of the area who had to find work in L-A also had to find housing near their jobs.

That's how the "Y Girls," as they called themselves, came together. They were sixteen- and seventeen-year-olds, and the YWCA in Lewiston was the place where they forged new bonds that have lasted a lifetime. Some of the Y Girls went to Bliss College. Others worked at the Armour & Co. meatpacking plant, at the Bates Mill or at the city's other textile mills.

Doris Carr Poole of Monmouth has coordinated their gatherings. The get-together several days ago included a visit by Louise Melanson Child, originally from Strong, who came from Brigham City, Utah. Others at the reunion were Marion and Elizabeth Toncer of Lewiston, twins from the Livermore Falls area; Barbara Phillips Burbank of Auburn, originally from Strong; Catherine Woods Saunders, now of Hebron; and Bea Forbes Lowell, who lives in Newry and came to the YWCA from western Maine.

Their reunion began with the usual talk of health issues and the accomplishments of grandchildren. Before it ended, thoughts returned to the Lewiston of the early 1940s.

Several of the Y Girls had boyfriends and family members in the service. They recalled how they gave support to one another and managed to make some wonderful memories despite the difficult times.

Waiting for the young men at war to return was nerve-wracking and filled with disappointments. After brief training, the soldiers shipped out. One of the servicemen who had been sent to France was reassigned to Manila, but his quick trip back across the United States didn't allow for a visit to Lewiston.

The reunited Y Girls didn't dwell on misfortunes, and for the most part, their family members and boyfriends had returned.

The ladies laughed as they reminisced about donuts and graham cracker pie at the nearby Hayes Diner. They talked about going to the Priscilla Theatre located on Pine Street until a few years ago, and they recalled special occasions like birthdays that called for dining out at the high-class DeWitt Hotel. They also enjoyed Sunday night concerts in the park, which was just across the street from the YWCA's location at Pine and Bates Streets.

"We were allowed to use the kitchen at the Y for a few cents a month, because we couldn't afford to eat out all the time," Doris Poole remembered. The group paid one dollar a week for cooking privileges, and they purchased the least expensive foods they could find.

Trolley cars were still running in the Twin Cities at that time, and the Y Girls sometimes went to Crowley's Junction for Saturday night dances. Servicemen from the Brunswick area came to the dances.

Curfew was 11:00 p.m., and the residence director (they fondly called her "Mother Hen") would enforce the rule with some occasional leniency.

Summing up for all, Doris Poole said, "What a wonderful experience it was."

SPECTACULAR BALLOONS OVER L-A

Every summer since 1992, the Great Falls Balloon Festival has been bringing crowds to the Twin Cities. The Androscoggin River is a beautiful backdrop for the August weekend launches of thirty to forty state-of-the-art hot air balloons, including a few large, special-shape balloons. Weather permitting, balloons lift off for morning and late afternoon flights, and the festival grounds are packed with people enjoying music on several stages, dozens of craft and food booths and exciting activity as crews prepare for ascents.

A group of local businesspeople started the festival with the intent of boosting business in the Twin Cities, benefitting nonprofit organizations and promoting Lewiston-Auburn as a tourist destination. It draws about 100,000 visitors annually, and the area's restaurants and hotels fill up rapidly.

A sky full of gigantic colorful balloons is a spectacular sight, but the Great Falls Balloon Festival flights were not the first time balloon ascensions caught the public's eye.

A balloon named *City of Lewiston* ascended from the City Park on the Fourth of July 1870. Tens of thousands of onlookers gathered for the marvelous event. That balloon originated in Lynn, Massachusetts. Parker Wells, a watchmaker and jeweler there, made it himself, although he had no balloon-making skills. It was cotton fabric, oiled and varnished, and it measured thirty-five feet in diameter and sixty feet in height. When flown in Lynn on the Fourth of July 1867 and 1868, it was decorated with an Eagle and named *City of Lynn*.

In 1869 and 1870, the balloon came to Lewiston. A detailed account of the 1870 holiday ascent appeared in the *Lewiston Evening Journal* on July 5, 1870. John Hall of Lynn, who had flown the balloon in Lynn, was its pilot here. He had made hundreds of ascents as a balloonist for the Army of the Potomac, and those feats were reported as follows:

> *For three years he interviewed the aerial spirits by night as well as by day, almost daily, bringing back to General Grant precious secrets of Lee's nimble movements—secrets which without difficulty he wrestles from the patriotic sky.*

The story explained that a connection was made to the pipes of the Lewiston Gas Co., and it took three hours for ten thousand cubic feet of the highly explosive natural gas to inflate the balloon. It had been a showery day, but the park continued to fill with spectators, and when liftoff occurred, it was estimated that thirty-five thousand people were present.

"It is doubtful that on eight acres of Pine Tree soil there ever were so many persons gathered before," the reporter wrote.

As the buoyancy increased, Professor Hall, as he was called, tied ropes from the balloon to a three-foot-diameter steel hoop, from which lines to the wicker passenger basket were attached. A long rope went straight up the top of the balloon to regulate an opening there. In the basket were seven fifty-pound bags of sand for ballast and an anchor on a rope.

The rain ended, and Hall cut the balloon free early in the evening. It rose quickly, with Hall "waving his handkerchief to the cheering multitude below." In still more flowery terms, the news story reported, "The splendid air-palace floats off between the spires of the City Building and the church" as the band struck up "The Star-Spangled Banner."

The balloon first moved off to the north and then eastward to the Sabattus and Wales area. "At just 8 p.m. the balloonist landed in Litchfield in a treetop, safe and sound," the paper noted.

Since those days, ascents have become a lot safer, and there's no better place to see these magnificent balloons than at the annual Great Falls Balloon Festival.

Always Labor Day Week

"Always Labor Day Week." That was a familiar slogan for the Maine State Fair about sixty years ago. At that time, the weeklong event was an occasion of excitement and wonder for a preteen boy like me. My family's Echo Farm on the North River Road in Auburn was directly across the river from the Lewiston Fairgrounds, and the racetrack announcements and carnival sounds filled the air for several days and nights.

FIRST
PREMIUM

MAINE
STATE
FAIR

1958

A blue ribbon received by an Echo Farm entry in the Maine State Fair.

I'm reminded of the Maine State Fair in Lewiston every time I walk out to our old barn in Auburn and look up at a cluster of multicolored prize ribbons tacked high on a rafter many years ago. There are red ribbons for second-place recognition, yellow and white for third and fourth and more than a few blue ribbons for first-place honors.

They hang there because my grandfather was very proud of the opportunity each year to exhibit the garden products of Echo Farm.

Anticipation of "Fair Week" began long before Labor Day. My father and grandfather had their eye on potential prizewinning squash and pumpkins throughout the summer. One of my grandfather's tactics for promoting their growth was to water the plants with lots of surplus milk from the dairy barn.

They took special care in preparation of garden entries. It was serious business, and they selected only the best ears of corn and the most perfect tomato and potato for display. Flowers were also cut and arranged. Often, the vase was a simple milk bottle, but the colorful late summer bouquets captured their share of prizes.

Every year, my grandfather hoped to come up with a spectacular sunflower specimen, and his entries came from plants that approached twelve feet, with seed-filled flowers the size of turkey platters.

My grandmother entered her needlework every year, too. I remember her beautiful hand-sewn quilt with postage stamp–sized squares that won her a blue ribbon.

The cool, dark cellar was safe storage for the vegetable harvests and preserved goods. My grandmother, Hattie Sargent, proudly displays the bounty.

Fancy needlework won a Maine State Fair blue ribbon for my grandmother, Hattie Sargent. Her quilt has hundreds of postage stamp–sized squares, all stitched together by hand.

The World of Mirth carnival played in Lewiston over many years at the fairgrounds and other locations. In 1957 and 1958, the show was paired with the Maine State Fair. Thousands of fun-seekers passed beneath a towering orange gate advertising the "Largest Midway on Earth."

"Hurry, Hurry. It's all inside. Alive, Alive!"

That kind of ballyhoo echoed through the so-called mile-long midway at the Lewiston Fairgrounds when the World of Mirth show was in town. In 1957 and 1958, the show was paired with the "Always Labor Day Week" Maine State Fair. Although it played earlier summer engagements in other years, I still link it with the fair.

Carnivals and fairs always were, and still are, a strange juxtaposition—the weirdest of sideshows, racy dancers and thinly veiled con games next to exhibition halls for grandma's quilts and apple pies.

During World of Mirth days in Lewiston—whether fair week or earlier—thousands of fun-seekers passed beneath the towering

Contests of oxen pulling and draft horse pulling were popular events at the Maine State Fair.

orange entrance gate of the show that was advertised as the "Largest Midway on Earth." In its heyday, it arrived on fifty railroad cars. Memorable features were a *Dancing Waters* lighted fountain show, jazz revues and exotic dancers—and several politically incorrect shows by today's standards.

There were two or three huge Ferris wheels. Some other rides were the Octopus, Tilt-A-Whirl, Round-Up, Chair-O-Plane and lots of kiddie rides.

Games of chance abounded, and somehow I always thought I could snare a camera with the Pitch-Til-U-Win hoops.

Our farm is directly across the Androscoggin River, and the World of Mirth's signature searchlights pierced the night sky. For several nights we heard the midway music and the screech of the motorcycle motodrome siren from the fairgrounds.

The World of Mirth didn't always play at the fairgrounds. Garcelon Field on Sabattus Street was an early location, and it was there that some exceptional events took place.

The show had a bull elephant named Teddy, and in addition to exhibition, he was animal power for midway work. In July 1941, Teddy demonstrated some bad behavior in Lewiston. He staged a minor rampage, upsetting automobiles with his five-foot tusks and refusing to submit to his handlers.

An account in a book by Bob Goldsack, *World of Mirth Shows: A Remembrance*, says that a boy from the monkey show was used as a decoy. Teddy was lured to a corral of wagons, where buckets of water were placed. When Teddy stopped to drink, workers quickly clamped cables on his legs.

In October, after a similar scene in Raleigh, North Carolina, Teddy came to a sad end when the show's owners ordered the elephant's destruction.

Wild weather hit the World of Mirth on September 16, 1943, when a "miniature tornado" ripped through the Garcelon Field midway. Goldsack's book says that show tents and large canvas posters were ripped to shreds and wagons were overturned.

The World of Mirth's first Lewiston appearance was in 1938, and its final show was in 1961.

My grandfather, Frederic Sargent (right), stands next to a display of modern machinery as he holds a hand scythe he had swung for thousands of hours.

In 1952, during the ninety-seventh Maine State Fair, the Lewiston Fairgrounds welcomed a particularly prominent visitor. Richard Nixon, on a vice-presidential campaign swing through Maine, stopped to shake some hands. B.J. Atwood of Sabattus and Clyde Luce of Farmington were two of the livestock exhibitors he greeted.

That year's fair featured the usual harness racing and musical revue in front of the large covered grandstand, but there was other competition about a mile away. Tommy Dorsey and his orchestra were booked for a "back-to-school hop" at the Lewiston Armory.

The Lewiston Fairgrounds was also the site of stock car races in the 1950s, as well as auto daredevil shows and a series of midget race car events.

On September 6, 1980, about 130,000 Deadheads descended on Lewiston (population 30,000) when the legendary Grateful Dead band appeared in a remarkable concert that went through the afternoon and into the evening, accompanied by a spectacular sunset.

It was an astonishing event for local people. A recent Internet post from one of the attendees reads, "Between sales and theft, the stores broke about even."

Agricultural fairs were held in Lewiston as early as 1837. The Maine State Agricultural Society began holding a state fair annually in 1855

The Lewiston Fairgrounds hosted the Maine State Fair for many years. This exhibition hall stood there in the early years before fire destroyed it.

and rotated them to venues around the state until a park was built in Lewiston. The first fair to use the grounds next to the railroad tracks on upper Main Street in Lewiston came in 1881, and visitors jammed the Twin Cities from all over New England.

The harness racing track is gone, and the large grandstand is only a memory. There was a big exhibition hall near the Main Street entrance. That hall was one of the first important elements of the fairgrounds to disappear. It was lost to fire around the middle of the last century.

St. Dom's Arena and the Great Fight

Even before the historic Cassius Clay–Sonny Liston heavyweight championship boxing match of 1965, the Birch Street area of Lewiston had a significant claim to fame in the world of sports.

It was the site of St. Dom's Arena, a community building that grew from extraordinary volunteer efforts. Although hockey on its ice rink was a major focal point, basketball fans will remember some great events that took place there on a remarkable wooden floor—the largest of its kind in the world.

Construction of St. Dom's Arena began in the late 1940s. By 1951, an ice plant had been installed, bringing indoor hockey to Twin Cities' fans. The building hosted other events, and around 1955, it also had a brand-new portable hardwood floor that was bigger than any other similar floor by some one hundred square feet.

Walter Brown, founder of the Boston Celtics and manager of Boston Garden, was a hockey fan first and foremost, and he had a financial hand in the construction of St. Dom's Arena. The floor was one of the last additions to the building before a major fire broke out and destroyed it on a Sunday morning in November 1956.

The Boston Celtics, featuring Coach Red Auerbach and standout Bob Cousy, played exhibition games on that portable floor and on a replacement that became a part of the Central Maine Youth Center (CMYC) when it was reconstructed in the late 1950s.

Roger P. Saucier wrote a detailed account of early Lewiston hockey and the history of St. Dom's Arena in a program published for the CMYC dedication on January 17, 1959. He goes all the way back to a 1916 article in the French-language newspaper *Le Messager*:

> *On Sunday afternoon, January 26, 1916, the people of Lewiston and Auburn witnessed the first hockey game ever played in this city. The game took place on the Association St. Dominique (ASD) rink on Bartlett Street in ideal weather and attracted a crowd of 300 interested sportsmen and women. The Association St. Dominique Club blanked the visiting Metropolitan Club of Auburn by a 7–0 score.*

Not only was St. Dom's hockey off to a historic start, but *Le Messager* also reported a day later that, in February 1916, Bates College was to play its first-ever hockey game against Bowdoin College on a new Bates College rink.

Those games were played outdoors, of course, so the construction of the massive St. Dom's Arena nearly forty years later was an exceptional undertaking and a major factor in the history of local hockey. The loss of the arena in that catastrophic fire is still felt deeply by many local residents.

Later years brought more hockey fame to the rebuilt CMYC, also called the Central Maine Civic Center and now known as the Androscoggin Bank Colisée.

The Maine Nordiques were the primary tenants at the Civic Center from 1973 to 1977. That colorful team had a cast of characters right out of the movie *Slap Shot*, according to the Colisée website. They were members of the old North American Hockey League, and in the end, it was the demise of the league itself that cut the Nordique era short.

The Lewiston MAINEiacs, a junior ice hockey team of the Quebec Major Junior Hockey League (QMJHL), came in 2003, and their history is still being written.

However, the area high schools have been the longest continuous tenants of the building that followed St. Dom's Arena in 1958. The strong showing of Lewiston and St. Dom's High Schools has resulted in several state and New England high school championships through the years.

I was a cub reporter for the *Lewiston Daily Sun* in the early 1960s, and I vividly recall the excitement that gripped the Twin Cities in weeks leading up to a controversial heavyweight title fight between Cassius Clay and Sonny Liston. I was assigned to interview Liston when he arrived at the airport, and though he had a fearsome reputation, I saw a playful side of him at that time.

He carried a box of chocolates in his huge hand, and his eyes twinkled when he saw an opportunity to open the box and offer a chocolate to someone. As the pleased party reached a hand into the box, Liston would press a button and set off a buzzer. He roared with delight as surprised victims shrieked and jumped away.

I attended the weigh-in at the Central Maine Youth Center prior to the fight and was able to snap some photos of Clay and Liston, as well as of Jersey Joe Walcott, the referee, and Robert Goulet, the noted singer who had family connections to Lewiston and gained notoriety when he flubbed the words to the national anthem on fight night.

Left: I interviewed heavyweight boxer Sonny Liston when he arrived a few days before his famous match in Lewiston against Cassius Clay, soon to be known as Muhammad Ali.

Below: I photographed the brash antics of Muhammad Ali, at the time still known as Cassius Clay, at the weigh-in a day before the fight on May 25, 1965.

My assignment on the night of May 25, 1965, was to make runs with staff photographers' film back to the newspaper office and the darkroom. When I arrived for the first batch of film, I learned that the fight was already over. Clay had thrown what would become known as his "phantom" punch within the first two minutes of the first round.

That fight and its many strange circumstances will forever be associated with Lewiston. There's another name that is synonymous with boxing in Lewiston, and that is Joey Gamache, whose exceptional skills and love of boxing brought him three world lightweight boxing crowns in the 1990s.

GOLF AT POLAND SPRING

Every so often, this part of the country grabs the world's attention, and sometimes it's the sports world that gets to know a little more about what makes our region so special.

No, it's not the 1965 Ali-Liston fight in Lewiston I'm talking about. It's golf. It was a world-class matchup, and it took place in 1900 at the new and beautiful course at nearby Poland Spring, a famous resort for the rich and famous a century ago.

At a time when Scottish professionals dominated American golf, Arthur Fenn was hailed as one of America's first homebred golfers. As an amateur, he won many championships, and when invited to design a course at Poland Spring, he quickly accepted. It was to be America's first course at a resort. The first six holes opened in 1893, and Fenn added three more holes later.

Fenn was recognized as one the United States' top golfers, but the real superstar of the day was Harry Varden. By 1900, Varden had won three British Opens in the past five years, and he would win two more.

The A.G. Spalding sports equipment firm was marketing a new golf ball called the Varden Flyer, and the company's tour to promote the ball brought Varden to Poland Spring.

That visit by "the greatest golfer in the world" became Maine's athletic event of the year. Exhibition matches were set up, including a mid-

August pairing with Fenn, who had become Poland Spring's resident pro. The match was being called "one of the greatest golf matches played in America." Hotel patrons wagered on whether Varden would be able to hit a three-hundred-yard drive on the sixth hole or whether he could shoot a thirty-six for the course.

A large gallery followed the golfers on that day. They endured an intense rainstorm, but Varden's play lived up to expectations. He narrowly beat Fenn and lowered the course record for both nine and eighteen holes.

According to descriptions of those early days of golf at Poland Spring, the sport caught on quickly, and the hotel's wealthy patrons appreciated its genteel qualities. The course scorecard emphasized etiquette and spelled out the game's special terminology.

In his book, *Poland Spring: A Tale of the Gilded Age, 1860–1900*, David L. Richards says that Poland Spring's trendy summer residents could send to Lewiston for the proper attire—golf suits, boots, stockings, belts and white duck trousers. Other fashionable wear included red golf coats and sweaters, plain and vested capes, fancy flannels and knit waistcoats from Boston.

Hill-Top, the resort's newspaper, said that golf at Poland Spring "has been a great thing for the plaid manufacturers." The newspaper advertised silver scoring pencils, gold golf pins, leather scorebooks and silver prize cups from Tiffany and Company of New York City.

Some of the celebrities who have played the Poland Spring course include baseball's legendary Babe Ruth; golf greats Walter Hagen, Bobby Jones and Ben Hogan; political patriarch Joseph Kennedy; Rockefellers; Roosevelts; and entertainers, including Jack Paar and Martin Milner.

In fact, Sonny Liston also played the course when he brought his entire training camp to Poland Spring prior to the 1965 championship fight.

If I had some kind of memory rewind, I'd go back to the senior banquet of the Edward Little High School class of 1958. It was held at the magnificent Poland Spring House.

We marveled at the opulence of this historic resort. As we entered, we were astonished by the massive two-hundred-foot-long dining room with windows that showcased the White Mountains.

The famous Poland Spring House was the summer destination of the rich and famous in America's Gilded Age. It burned down in 1975.

We joked about proper etiquette in such a place. We puzzled over finger bowls and an array of flatware. We knew which classmates were probably more comfortable in such a place and which were not.

The efficient corps of uniformed waitresses made us feel like sophisticated men and women of the world, but I'm sure there were lots of laughs about our ill-concealed awkwardness when they got behind the kitchen doors.

Now, looking back, I realize I was mostly unaware of the grandeur of the Gilded Age at Poland Spring. It really didn't hit me that I was dining where presidents had dined. It was here that Rose and Joe Kennedy honeymooned. Babe Ruth had been here, and Betty Grable, Mae West, Joe Lewis, Judy Garland.

Decades before the movie stars came, the resort catered to the elite of Boston and New York.

The Poland Spring House dining room offered a grand setting for the lovely gowns of the early 1900s. They were lavishly trimmed in laces, and many had long trains. The length of the dining room, and the carpeted runner, provided the perfect backdrop for the display of these creations, and some ladies specifically requested tables at the far end of the dining room so they could display their finery as they strolled elegantly down its full length.

Meals were a lavish affair with numerous courses. The menu for Sunday, September 28, 1884, offered three soups, fish, three boiled meats, five roasts, four cold dishes, four entrees, ten vegetables, eleven relishes, four pastries and twelve desserts, plus tea and coffee.

The coffee was nothing but Chase and Sanborn blend—probably because James S. Sanborn of the famous company owned Elmwood Farm in Poland, where he raised champion horses.

I wish I could remember the details of our senior class menu, and I wonder if our meal was served on the hotel's custom-made ironstone china with the Poland Spring name and the Ricker Family crest. This china came in a variety of sizes and shapes, ranging from tiny demitasse cups and saucers to large round and oval plates for meat and fish courses. Five different sizes of round plates were used.

By 1958, the wonderful resort had actually been in decline under absentee ownership for twenty years. We couldn't foresee then that it would close a few years later and then would undergo a series of sad changes as the federal government turned it into the largest women's Job Corps facility in the country. The history-haunted rooms and halls were remodeled to conform to government regulations.

A tragic fire leveled the Poland Spring House on July 3, 1975, just one day before its ninety-ninth anniversary.

"ROUGH" CARRIGAN AND THE RED SOX

Summer and baseball go together, and the success of the Boston Red Sox in recent years is fresh enough to keep everyone talking about the team's chances. After all, "the curse" has been broken.

Baseball is a sport of statistics, and time-honored stories turn trivia into legend. There's a Lewiston link to the Red Sox of nearly one hundred years ago that stands head and shoulders above many of the greatest accomplishments in the history of our national pastime.

William F. "Rough" Carrigan was a Lewiston native and one of the game's greatest managers. He was inducted into the Red Sox Hall of Fame almost forty years after his death here in 1969.

Carrigan was an outstanding catcher, but more importantly, he was the only manager to lead the Bosox to two World Series titles until Tony Francona matched that feat in 2007. His success took place before the celebrated "curse," when Babe Ruth went from the Red Sox to the New York Yankees.

Under Carrigan, the Red Sox finished second in 1914 and then won the world championships in 1915 and 1916. What followed after 1918 was a long dry spell of shattered hopes for Red Sox fans.

The son of a storekeeper, Carrigan was born in Lewiston in 1883. It was his older brother, John, a promising pitcher, who started the boy on the road to diamond fame. He convinced young Bill to be his practice catcher until John was sidelined by injuries.

Bill gained local fame on sandlot fields and at Lewiston High School, where he also excelled in football. He even played roller-polo, a kind of hockey played on roller skates. His brother persuaded Bill to give it up because of the many fights he got into.

In his prep school and college years, Bill sustained a football injury that limited his speed, and his full potential, when he got to the Major Leagues. Carrigan replaced Red Sox starting catcher Lou Criger soon after signing a contract in 1906. In his first year, he was one of the catchers in the longest game in American League history: twenty-four innings against the Philadelphia Athletics. An interesting fact about that long game is that the A's pitcher was "Iron Man Jack" Coombs of Freeport, Maine.

Carrigan also had the distinction of catching three no-hit games.

He replaced Jack Stahl as Red Sox manager halfway through the 1913 season. In 1914, Babe Ruth joined the Sox. The Babe was a wild party animal, and in order to keep the Red Sox prize pitcher under control, Carrigan made himself Ruth's roommate. One night, Ruth snuck out and got himself arrested, according to an account in *Magnificent Mainers*, a book by Jeff Hollingsworth. Carrigan refused to post bail.

Hollingsworth reported that Carrigan said, "I'll bail him out tomorrow morning. That way, I'll know where he will be for tonight."

In a series of articles he wrote for the *Boston Daily Record*, Carrigan recalled:

> *Nobody could have made Ruth the great pitcher and the great hitter he was but himself. He made himself with the aid of his God-given talents. But, breaking in, he had to be disciplined to save him from probably becoming his own worst enemy. And I saw to it that he was disciplined.*

Carrigan's nickname—"Rough"—was well earned, and his square jaw with a Kirk Douglas cleft made him look the part. Nevertheless, he was regarded as being fair. He also was known as "the Human Stone Wall" for his ability to block opposing runners, sometimes sitting right on home plate. He once taunted Ty Cobb with, "Come on, you. Steal. I dare you. Just try!"

In 1916, Carrigan retired to a career in banking in Maine. Although he returned to manage the Red Sox in 1927, he couldn't recapture the former glory. Boston finished last for three seasons in a row.

Bill Carrigan died in Lewiston at the age of eighty-five.

The next time some Lewiston fans travel to a game at Fenway Park, I hope they tell everyone near them about the days of Bill "Rough" Carrigan from Lewiston, Maine.

WALLINGFORD'S POWDER MAKER AND TOWER GUNS

Every four years, I'm reminded how much the winter Olympic games owe to Auburn, its diminutive Lost Valley Ski Area and the inventive genius of the late Otto Wallingford. When Mother Nature doesn't provide, ski slopes around the world can count on quality snow whenever and wherever they need it, thanks to something Wallingford started about fifty years ago on that 240-foot-high hill near Young's Corner.

It was 1962 when Wallingford blew the first snow from his own ingenious machinery. He went on to tweak his system with the first air dryer and fashioned the first pole guns—now called tower guns—by mounting hoses twenty feet above the trail to simulate natural snowfall. We now call them tower guns, and they are essential components of snowmaking around the globe.

What came out of those early guns was more like ice bullets than snow, but that just led Wallingford to further refinements that made possible the white-carpet grooming we now take for granted. Wallingford invented the Powder Maker, which used a giant roller with openings like a chain-link fence. When dragged at an angle, it would pulverize hardpack into soft, carveable snow.

That hill in Auburn with Maine's first man-made snow helped produce some Olympic greats.

Julie Parisien, who grew up in Auburn and was a member of the 1992 Olympic ski team, has talked fondly of her early training at Lost Valley.

She became a three-time Olympian (1992 in Albertville, France; 1994 in Lillehammer, Norway; and 1998 in Nagano, Japan) along with her younger sister Anna (1994) and brother Rob (1992). She is the first person ever (male or female) to be ranked number one in the world both as an amateur and professional. She won three World Cups, finished fourth in the 1992 Olympic competition at Albertville and won a silver medal at the 1993 World Championships. In the 1991 U.S. Championships, Parisien won gold in Super G and silver in downhill, and she continues to work closely with Maine children to install values she learned in winter sports.

Before Lost Valley, there was Pettengill Park in Auburn, with its towering ski jump, where John Bower began soaring to greatness. Bower first jumped into record books with a perfect four hundred when he won slalom, downhill, cross country and jumping in a high school championship in 1959. A few years later, Auburn and Maine couldn't have been prouder of its native son when Bower became the first American to win the Holmenkollen King's Cup in Norway in 1968. It was then the world's most coveted combined Nordic event.

As a U.S. Nordic team member, he competed in two Olympics (1964 in Innsbruck, Austria; and 1968 in Grenoble, France) and won four national

Nordic combined titles. Bower later coached at Middlebury College and the U.S. Nordic team. He went on to manage winter sports venues in Park City, Utah, and he was involved in the winter Olympics there. His son, Ricky Bower, is a name known to snowboarders worldwide. Ricky has won half-pipe world championships and was featured in a film documentary called *Pipe Dreams*. Ricky went to Italy as a coach of the U.S. snowboarders in the Torino Olympics.

Pettengill Park also was the site of the Nordic skiing trails that would lead Tom Upham to Olympic competition in Grenoble in 1968.

It's a small world, and we live in one of the best parts of it.

For those of us who never reached Olympic status, we still remember sliding on Pettengill's hill and skating in the 1950s under the lights to music from the loudspeaker of the warming shack. If it was a snowy day or night, high school boys grabbed shovels and, in line across the ice, made quick work of clearing it.

These memories of locations in Auburn and champions with Auburn ties are most vivid in my mind, but Lewiston people and places also figure importantly in the winter lore of the Twin Cities.

There were spectacular snowshoe club events that reached their peak half a century ago. Lewiston came vibrantly alive in midwinter as thousands of snowshoe club members gathered here.

Most snowshoers arrived by train from Canada on a Saturday morning at the Grand Trunk station on Lincoln Street. Others came from Biddeford and Rumford. The festivities centered on an ice palace built in a Lewiston location for each convention. The massive ice-block structures were often in City Park (long before it was Kennedy Park) or at Hulett Square (at Main and Lisbon Streets).

Weekend snowshoe races and a parade showcased colorful costumes and, often, colorful behavior. Bands played, choral performances were held and groups organized stunts such as blanket tossing (launching someone high in the air from a blanket held by about a dozen people).

The Sunday morning parade ended with mass at Saints Peter and Paul Church, which is now Maine's only basilica.

Basketball in a Cage

Basketball in a cage. Now, that sounds like the latest idea for an extreme sports event on cable TV. Actually, it's a fair description of what the holiday hoops season was like in Auburn almost one hundred years ago.

Basketball was a fairly new sport, and there weren't many indoor floors large enough for a wintertime game. The auditorium on the second floor of Auburn Hall fit the bill, with certain limitations. Some local athletes not long out of high school organized the Waseca Club, and their exploits gave Auburn a prominent place in Maine's basketball history.

It was pre–World War I, and the local schools had not yet adopted basketball for their sports schedules. Nevertheless, the game was developing a strong local following. Regulation dimensions were not a concern. The playing floor was almost square, and the foul lines were only about twenty feet apart. It wasn't uncommon for a good long shot to be made from the opposite foul line, and one-handed shots were often tried from the full length of the court, which wasn't more than forty-five or fifty feet. (Today's NBA court is ninety-four by fifty feet.)

The hall was upstairs over three stores, and the entrance was at the upper west end. There was just one flight of stairs about twelve feet wide, and the ticket office was at the top. A policeman guarded the door to the hall, and he also served as the ticket taker.

When fans entered the hall, they faced an arrangement of netting that formed a kind of cage. Inside this cage was the playing area, and the net kept the ball from landing in the balcony and slowing up the game.

It was a structure similar to hockey rink sideboards, made in fifteen-foot sections and held end-to-end by large screw eyes and latches. The sideboard barrier reached from the hall's stage down one side of the hall, across the hall, and up the other side, with the stage forming the fourth side. Fans at floor level were on settees behind the net.

Legend has it that the cage idea was suggested during meetings of the Waseca Social Club as a joke, but a plan soon took root. Ray H. Thayer of Auburn, manager of the Wasecas, and his assistant, Herbert Gammon, get credit for design and construction of the cage.

Fans loved it. The cage allowed almost continual play for the ten- or twelve-minute periods.

It must have been a remarkable experience to be at Auburn Hall in those days. The following descriptions come from a 1968 *Lewiston Evening Journal* feature story by Dick Murray, who had vivid memories of the colorful Auburn Hall crowd fifty or more years earlier. He recalled how a youngster without a ticket could sometimes find a softhearted player to get him in. The player would let the kid carry his equipment bag past the policeman. Crowds were packed in shoulder-to-shoulder, and the cheering was nonstop. Fights broke out here and there, sometimes spilling over into the play area. As soon as the game ended, volunteers quickly removed the cage, and a five- or six-piece orchestra would set up for the after-the-game dance.

It was a raucous, rambunctious gathering at Auburn Hall on those Friday nights.

About the Author

David A. Sargent is a native of Auburn, Maine. Raised on the farm built by his great-grandfather after the Civil War, he has pursued a lifelong interest in writing and history built on the Maine-flavored poetry and journalism of his father; his brother, Jim; and an aunt. He was a general assignment reporter for the *Lewiston Daily Sun* in the 1960s, worked for a public relations company in Portland and operated his own PR firm. He was communications manager for a Maine paper industry trade association, and in recent years, he founded, edited and published *Business Focus*, a monthly newspaper. He lives with his wife, Judy, on the historic family farm. They have two daughters and six grandchildren. His columns, "River Views," have appeared twice monthly in the *Lewiston Sun Journal* since 2005.

Visit us at
www.historypress.net